# 33 Annual
# Wild and Wacky
# Holiday-ish
# Occasions

## You Never Knew
## You Wanted to Celebrate!

By Rita Beck

CreateSpace Independent Publishing Program

Cover and interior design by Rita Beck

Clipart used by license permission:
123RF, Shutterstock, Can Stock Photos

Genre: Humor & Entertainment

# Dedication

*To my awesome husband, Eric,*
*for his love, his support, his patience,*
*his humor and his cooking.*

# Contents

## November

## December

# Introduction

*33 Annual Wild & Wacky Holidays-ish Occasions – You Never Knew You Wanted to Celebrate* is a book about wild, happy, quirky, wacky, silly, weird, and sometimes rowdy holiday-*ish* days, weeks and anniversaries! There are literally dozens of these imitations for celebrations found in every single month and many have been around and celebrated for decades!

Designed to be a coffee table gift book and/or stocking stuffer, 33 Annual Wild and Wacky Holiday-ish Occasions is a perfect gift for that person who has everything they need, but you gotta get them a gift anyway, type of gift. You know, people like your boss, your teacher, your grandmother, your college roommate, your favorite bartender, your Aqua Zumba instructor, your corporate event planner, yourself.

It's an amusing, and sometimes comical go-to resource that you can browse through every month for fun, festive and informative news about special holiday-*ish* days you can celebrate, commemorate, or just plain contemplate. Browse this book whenever you want for news you can use to amuse for Facebook, theme parties, class projects, family activities, newsletters, fun at work, or for conversation pieces when you're squished like a sardine on the subway.

*33AWWHO* highlights holiday-like days that most people never knew existed. Why write a book about holiday impersonators? Because most people love holidays—the more the merrier! We get to celebrate, we let loose, we get happy, we make memories!

But holidays come and go, and then many of us often wait impatiently for the next one to come along, simply because our day-to-day lives can be far from festive. And then we hear on the radio or on social media that today is one of those quirky, but increasingly trendy fake holidays like *Belly Laugh Day* (Jan.) or *Spunky Old Broads Day* (Feb.) or *Wonderful Weirdos Day* (Sep.), and some of us think, "Now that's something I could celebrate!

Well, believe it or not, there's a whole heap of hidden holiday-*ish* days one can pay homage to in every single month, every single year! Some are quaint, some are peculiar, and some are downright bizarre. There are oodles of these days of wonder, created by people to encourage other people to celebrate their special purpose. Many are commemorated as national holiday-*ish* days, and more than a few are celebrated worldwide.

*33AWWHO* is not your daddy's run-of-the-mill list of unusual observances that include all those warm and fuzzy days like "Grandparents Day" or "Take Your Teddy Bear to Work Day." You won't see hordes of boring food days either, like "National Eggplant Day." Cute as they are, they're far too tame for this book's collection which focuses on the bolder and funkier days like *Nothing Like a Dame Day* (Apr.), along with some of the more civilized observances like *Talk Like Shakespeare Day* (also Apr.), to the more rowdy, let's-have-a-party days like *National Chicken Dance Day* (May).

This book doesn't just mention a bunch of peculiar proclamations, it delves into their purpose and their origins, then highlights examples of how you can join the many thousands of fun-loving people who like to celebrate, commemorate, or just plain contemplate these amazing days. Each page is sprinkled with chuckle-worthy commentary and fun factoids meant to engage you with a lively piece of entertainment that is enlightening, inspiring, quite often empowering, and well worth sharing with others so that fun can be had by all!

All wacky holidays featured in *33AWWHO* have been documented and legitimized either by being listed in *Chase's Calendar of Events* (the *official* guide to holidays), or by being featured dozens of times web-wide. Greeting card companies have joined in on the fun to honor some of the wackiest occasions with e-cards.

Also, be sure to check out the trending Twitter Hashtags that go active every year for all or most of the 33AWWHO, like #SerendipityDay and #StupidGuyThingDay. Browse the Twitter Hashtag Index at the back of this book, and if you find one you like that isn't active, then that's your cue to make it happen. Many of these special occasions have their own Facebook pages and websites where you can easily search for local and national annual celebrations and events. If you're looking for something *really* bold and brave and empowering, visit GoToplessDay.com. Always a fan favorite.

Share this book with friends and family, or better yet, buy them a copy! If you give this one a prominent place on your coffee table, I guarantee you it will be the most popular item there ... as long as you don't start using it as a coaster. Remember to browse each month to see what's coming up. Breeze through a few pages during those long commercials on TV or read some to the family during breakfast so everyone can create and plan and pick teams for a holiday-themed game night.

Before you know it, you'll have read about all 33 days of fun, and then it'll be time to go back and pick and choose all the wild and wacky holiday-*ish* occasions in the *New Year* that you never knew you wanted to celebrate, commemorate, or just plain contemplate!

Rita Beck

# JANUARY

## Is Way More Than Just a Welcome Mat
## For a Happy New Year!

At the end of a long and festive holiday season, January is usually a time to put away all of our celebratory hats, hangovers, credit cards and Christmas trees for a long, hibernating, holiday hiatus. Good riddance to all those days of holly—it's time to settle into winter's melancholy. Or is it? Some of us may still be filled with the holiday spirit and are not quite ready to unwrap ourselves from the gift of cheerful glee that the holiday season tends to bring.

What does one do when they're reluctant to relinquish their happy holidays because of all the holly, jolly and joy they have left over? Well, as it happens, January has a whole host of hidden wild, wacky and happy holiday-*ish* occasions one could consider paying homage to. January is way more than just a welcoming mat for a Happy New Year. It actually features a vast array of not only happy, wild and wacky days, but wacky weeks as well!

\* \* \*

# Someday We'll Laugh About This Week

## Always January 2-8

## New Year's Resolutions
## We Can All Laugh About

*Someday We'll Laugh About This Week* is a special annual occurrence designed to fill us with mirth for seven whole days! What have you, personally, got to laugh about? Well, you can probably laugh yourself silly about all the New Year's resolutions you know you'll break even before the Christmas decorations are packed away. That's what *Someday We'll Laugh About*

*This Week* is really all about—90 percent of our purposeful proclamations are pitched within the first week of the New Year. *(Well, you gotta be good at something, right?)*

The health and financial-related resolutions are usually the first to be rescinded. Like when you resolve to exercise more, eat less, save more, spend less, get out of debt or cry tryin'. Sound laughingly familiar? Well, feel free to LOL over all those failed resolutions—all week long! So what if you made an irrevocable resolution to lose ten pounds, but you've already gained eight because of all that you have managed to devour since Thanksgiving, including an entire gingerbread house the size of a multi-unit apartment building! *Someday We'll Laugh About This Week* means it's perfectly acceptable to laugh at yourself and to even celebrate your failures.

> *This week says it's perfectly acceptable to laugh at yourself and to even celebrate your failures.*

Since many of us are still hungover from all the celebratory activities connected to New Year's Eve, consider celebrating *Someday We'll Laugh About This Week* via anything other than a party. Consider gathering at the beginning of the week with your family and/or friends over dinner or social media and collaborate together to create and share all your New Year's resolutions. Then get together again at the end of *Someday We'll Laugh About This Week*, and compare. Anyone who still has 100% of their New Year's resolutions intact and on track wins!

If that's too easy, then extend the end date to one month, or even 6 months if that's how long it takes to get a winner. And think about it. This little exercise in will power and discipline could easily morph into a very healthy and fun competition.

Some people prefer to commemorate this annual occasion by looking at the new year as a fresh new start. Others contemplate the occasion, and then they click the refresh button on their old bad habits. Then they just laugh at all the other folks who keep beating themselves up over all the shoulda-woulda-couldas that ultimately ended in a bunch of "Whatevers!"

Still not sure if you have anything to laugh about? Well, many of us can probably laugh with unceasing hilarity when we see our holiday shopping credit card bills. Or, if "stop procrastinating" is one of the New Year's resolutions you're pretty sure is gonna get pitched pretty soon, then wait until January 24th— that's *Belly Laugh Day (covered in a few pages.)* And if you're absolutely positive you're gonna break most of your New Year's resolutions, try resolving to get fat and lazy and to max out all your credit cards and see what happens!

*"May all your troubles last as long as your New Year's resolutions."* ~Joey Adams

> *"May all your troubles last as long as your New Year's resolutions."*
> ~Joey Adams

\* \* \*

# Hunt for Happiness Week

Always the 3rd Week in January

## Hunt for the Happiness
## That is Hiding in Plain Sight

This week to seek happiness was actually conceived by *The Secret Society of Happy People.* You've probably never heard of the SSOHP, hence the word "secret" in their name, so mum's the word, OK? (Visit www.sohp.com if you're a glass-half-full kinda person and check out the *31 Types of Happiness* the members of this secret society live by.)

It's no secret, however, that many people experience post-holiday blues as the gloomy days of winter start to settle in. *Hunt for Happiness Week* was created to encourage us to actively seek the happy moments in our day-to-day lives, even among the chaos and stress and unpleasantness that can often engulf our world on a daily basis. It inspires us to seek and embrace some of the simple pleasures in life—it's a day when parade-raining of any kind is discouraged.

It's also no big secret that people often hunt for happiness in all the wrong places. Bars. Botox parties. Dairy Queen. Is that new $15,000 Prada handbag really going to bring you happiness? How about purchasing your very own Dairy Queen franchise? Is that truly going to make you happy? Some might say, "Heck, yeah! Happiness is where you find it!" And that's exactly right. But *Hunt for Happiness Week* is not about *buying* happiness, it's about finding happiness where you least expect it.

*Find the little things in your life that might inspire you to break into your happy dance.*

Our pursuit of happiness shouldn't always cost us anything, and it most often doesn't when we endeavor to seek and find happiness in the simple pleasures in life. But the fact is, even that can be easier said than done, right? Wrong! *Hunt for Happiness Week* was created to inspire us to look within ourselves to discover, and most importantly, to *recognize* the happy moments in our daily lives. And remember, it's "the little things in life" that we often take for granted, that have the ability to make us smile a happy smile.

Commemorate *Hunt for Happiness Week* by seeing how many little things in your life—throughout the entire 3rd week of January—you can string together that might inspire you to break into your happy dance. Feel free to borrow some of these...

- You still have all your teeth.
- Online shopping.
- Chocolate.
- All your kids are out of diapers.
- You're having a good hair week.
- Nobody in the family has ever been to prison.
- Beer.
- The unemployment rate went down again.
- Everyone in your family is free of cavities and lice.
- Your team won the big game.
- Ice Cream.
- You love your job and/or your neighbors.
- Netflix.
- Your Holiday Season wasn't the total "stress fest" you had anticipated.
- You can't remember the last time you received a call from a telemarketer.
- Bacon.
- Your kitten / hamster / ferret video went viral.
- Indoor plumbing.

*Happy Hunting, my friends!*

\* \* \*

# Belly Laugh Day

## Always January 24th

## Belly Laugh Day Bounces One Laugh All Around the World

*Belly Laugh Day* is a delightful day that was designed to bounce a belly laugh around the world! That's right folks, and it's apparently a huge event! Every year at 1:24PM, local time, on January 24th, people from Milwaukee to Malaysia, in schools, and factories, office buildings, and sports arenas, PEOPLE ALL AROUND THE WORLD will stop what they are doing, smile, throw their arms in the air and laugh out loud! What an incredibly awesome idea!

Whoever came up with this madcap moment of merriment is no doubt familiar with the health benefits of belly laughs. It's a natural medicine and it's quite contagious—just hearing laughter primes our brain and readies us to smile and join in on the fun. Some say that laughter is *God's* medicine. And more and more medical research studies agree that the "internal jogging" one gets from a good, hearty belly laugh triggers the release of endorphins—the body's natural feel-good chemicals.

> *Some say that laughter is God's medicine. And more and more medical research studies agree...*

Clinical studies using "laugh therapy" have proven that LOLing actually relieves stress, diminishes pain, improves our mood, boosts our energy, eases anxiety and fear, strengthens our immune system, and is said to even help protect us against cardiovascular problems. *(Wow, I feel better already!)*

Better yet, they say that after laughing for only a few minutes, you may feel better for hours. Laughter is not only free, it's fun, easy to use, and is like an instant vacation from whatever ails you.

Share some hilarity with someone you care about or check out www.BellyLaughDay.com to join the Belly Laugh Bounce Around the World on January 24th. Why not pay tribute to the day by spending the evening with friends and/or family watching old episodes of *Saturday Night Live, I Love Lucy* or *America's Funniest Home Videos*? Or movies like *Home Alone, Blazing Saddles* or *The Original Kings of Comedy*. Organize a BYOJ Contest (Bring Your Own Joke) day at work. Warning: Side effects of belly laughing may include uncontrollable weeping and peeing in pants.

*"I am thankful for laughter, except when milk comes out of my nose."* ~Woody Allen

✱ ✱ ✱

# Spunky Old Broads Day

## February 1st and All Month Long!

### It's Spunky Old Broads Day
### All Month Long!

So, there's actually a day for *Spunky Old Broads,* huh? How cool is that? And it was apparently *so* cool, it was decided that the entire month of February should be declared *Spunky Old Broads Month!* And that's beyond cool.

This official declaration is dedicated to geriatric divas everywhere—the ones who strut their stuff in t-shirts that say things like, "It Took Me 60 Years to Look This Good!" *Spunky Old Broads Day / Month* is a wild and wacky annual occasion in recognition of the gutsy Grandmas who say things like, "When I was young, I went braless in support of the women's liberation movement; now I go braless because it helps pull the wrinkles out of my face." Think Betty White or Whoopi Goldberg.

*SOB Day celebrates the women who believe that it's never too late to be what you've always wanted to be and/or do what you've always wanted to do.*

Do *Spunky Old Broads* deserve an entire month of recognition and celebration? Hell Yeah! *(Said the Spunky Old Broad.)* Ask any of the feisty old females you might know—there are plenty of them around. They're your mothers, your grandmothers, your neighbors, your Walmart greeters, your bosses, your crazy elderly aunt who claims she's a back-up dancer for Willie Nelson. In other words, these SOBs could be some of the most important people in your life, and it would behoove you to pay homage to them not only during all 28 days of February, but during any other month that has 28 days! *(That would be all of them.)*

The official objective of *Spunky Old Broads Day* and month pertains to all women over age 50 who are interested in living a regret-free life. It is my belief, however, that "regret" would definitely be felt by anyone who decides to call a spunky 50-year-old woman "old" to her face. You might be able to get away with that for a 60-year-old, but spunky or not, I don't know of any 50-year-old woman who thinks of herself as *old.* Heck, a 50-year-old ain't even old enough to be a Baby Boomer! They were all born between 1946-1964, and it's fair game to call Boomers old, but only because most of them are very proud to say that they're making it cool to grow old!

*Spunky Old Broads Day/Month* celebrates the women who believe that it's never too late to be what you've always wanted to be and/or do what you've always wanted to do. These are women who refuse to spend their days sitting quietly in rocking chairs because they'd rather be blasting some classic rock on the 8-track tape player in their classic 1965 Mustang convertible, as they take their annual road trip to Las Vegas, baby! And I can pretty much guarantee you that, back in the day, many of these old broads were directly connected to the reason someone had to come up with, "What happens in Vegas stays in Vegas."

So, if you happen to be an SOB looking to make your mark on the auspicious occasion of *SOB Day,* which, again, is *all month long,* some of the most popular suggestions for celebrating it range from mud wrestling to nude sky diving. I can't speak for all funky, flashy, although sometimes feeble females, but if I were going to wrestle, I would prefer to do it in Jell-O, especially since there's always tons of it at the retirement communities. And nude sky diving, to me, sounds like a cactus landing waiting to happen, so I wouldn't suggest that one either. But for spirited old girls who just wanna have fun, consider these lively and entertaining suggestions for celebration:

> *"Getting old ain't so bad. My wrinkles don't hurt one bit!"*

- Grab your single gal pals and go on a singles "cougar-themed" cruise. *(Yes, Agnes, I do believe those still exist.)*

- Organize teams for competitive games down at the Senior Center, like pickle ball, or strip pinochle.

- Have a booze and Botox party.

- Take your besties for a hot-air balloon ride.

- Pursue your passion to perform by putting together a stand-up comedy routine and posting it on YouTube.

- Start a Jell-O food fight with your grandkids.

- Decide to live life to the fullest regardless of your circumstances and share that spirit with those around you.

- Take up tap dancing or join a hip-hop exercise class.

- Plan a lively night with friends at the local male stripper joint.

- Order and wear t-shirts throughout the month that say things like: "Aged to Perfection," or "I'm still hot! It just comes in flashes."

- Take an annual SOB road trip to Vegas baby!! *(Where February temps average a balmy 60 degrees and the convertible Mustangs are just a car rental away.)*

- Put some *sassy* in your *classy* and decide to become a *Spunky Old Broad!*

If you're *not* an SOB, but want to pay homage to one of the frail, but fiery, semi-senile senior citizen(s) in your life, give her a gift that says you think *she's* aged to perfection—buy her a t-shirt, or throw pillow or an embroidered doily that says something like:

- "Old is the new black!"
- "Getting old ain't so bad. My wrinkles don't hurt one bit!"
- "I'm starting to think I'll never be old enough to know better!"
- "At my age, I can live without sex, but not without my reading glasses!"

*Have a Happy SOBs Day! All month long!*

# Dump Your Significant Jerk Day

Always the Week Before Valentine's Day

## 25 Great Break-up Lines for
## Dump Your Significant Jerk Day!

The first day of the week before Valentine's Day is *Dump Your Significant Jerk Day!* Yes, my friends, someone had the good sense to come up with a very special day designated for dumping significant others who have morphed into *significant jerks!* The fact that this special occasion occurs right before Valentine's Day makes the concept all the more ... efficient and effective. The icing on the cake of *Dump Your Significant Jerk Day* is that it kicks off *Dump Your Significant*

*Jerk Week* (always the week before Valentine's Day), allowing extended opportunities for Dumpers to disassemble their relationship with their Dumpees.

There's plenty of us—both women and men—who have either dated a jerk at some point, or—for some incredibly dumb reason—are currently dating a jerk. When a relationship has gone from incredibly divine to incredibly despicable, and Valentine's Day is just around the corner, many people find themselves incredibly desperate to dump their significant jerk. But dumping them before having to cough up cash for an official holiday that has been designated and celebrated for centuries as a day to show your love for said jerk, can prove to be incredibly problematic, and stressful.

*Effective and efficient dumping of significant jerks may require extensive planning, creativity, and/or rehearsals in front of a mirror.*

I can hear some women now, saying, "I should have listened to that so-called friend who introduced the two of us when they said, 'He's a good guy once you get to know him,' because what they really meant was, 'He's an incredible jerk, but you'll get used to it!'"

That's all water under the bridge now though, and even though many women had thoughts and visions of shoving their unworthy butthead boyfriend off a bridge or into the path of a speeding dump truck, those justifiable acts of satisfaction are still ... illegal. And *that*, my friends, is one of the dozens of reasons why some forward-thinking smart person came up with *Dump Your Significant Jerk Day*!

Believe it or not, this annual jerk-dumping occasion actually began almost 30 years ago. It was probably extended to a week-long event shortly thereafter because dumping jerks, particularly significant ones, can be easier said than

*"The village called. They'd like their idiot back. You'd better get going."*

done, and may take some time. Effective and efficient dumping of a significant jerk may require extensive planning, creativity, and/or rehearsals in front of a mirror, especially when pulling off a justifiable act of retribution that is both satisfying and still ... legal.

Some qualifying reasons that may make a relationship dump-worthy include, but are not limited to the fact that the arrangement has proven to be: unhappy, unfulfilling, unhealthy, unbearable, dysfunctional, disappointing, disastrous, or... all of the above.

In honor of this year's annual *Dump Your Significant Jerk Day / Week*, I have supplied the following list of 25 delightfully rewarding and gratifying break-up lines—some of the best me and the Internet have to offer—to help you find just the right things to say to all types of significant jerks in desperate need of dumping.

For significant "he" jerks...

1.  To the jerk you once wanted to marry, until you found his cheating was legendary, say...
    *"Remember that time I told you that I loved you? Well this is like that in no way. Buh-bye!"*

2.   Break the news to that boring boob-head who acts like he's brain dead...
*"The village called. They'd like their idiot back. You'd better get going."*

3.   Tell that cute, but way-too-controlling crazy person who calls you 22 times a day...
*"Is it hot in here, or is this relationship suffocating me? Here's the deal—it's been real! Bye Felicia!"*

4.   To the cheap creep you no longer want to keep...
*"Grab a straw, because you suck! Here's your coat—you are now just a footnote."*

5.   Declare to that dysfunctional dipstick who keeps stealing your lipstick...
*"I now pronounce you dumped and single. You may now kiss my ass."*

6.   Explain to your deadbeat Baby Daddy who you once thought was classy...
*"It's just that our time together has seriously become way more effort that you're worth. Oh, and I accidentally dropped your phone in the baby's poopy diaper."*

7.   Advise that handsome hotheaded bully with the oh-so-smokin' body...
*"You're the reason nobody likes you—you're a jackass! Later hater!"*

8.   For that cigarette-smoking mutton-head...
*"There are some remarkably dumb people in this world. Thanks for helping me understand that. Smell you later!"*

9. Notify that lyin', boozin', low-life loser that you once thought you loved...
*"You're like a hemorrhoid—a pain in the ass that won't go away. See ya. Wouldn't wanna be ya."*

10. Enlighten that kinky porn-addicted pinhead...
*"If God actually gave it some thought, I'm certain he could think of something better to do with skin rather than hold your sorry a\*s together. Amen."*

11. To that lamebrain meathead who lives in his mother's basement...
*"You're such a moron, you're living proof that man can live without a brain! Later Loser!"*

12. Inform that old farting fathead that you met down at the senior center...
*"You're so full of crap that you'll probably die of constipation, and I'm blowin' this popsicle stand!"*

13. Ask that bonehead with the bad sex...
*"If I threw a stick, you'd leave, right?"*

14. Confess to that always-negative nincom-poop...
*"I'm tired of you always pissing in my Cheerios! I've come to love the sound you make when you shut up. Peace out!"*

15. Say to that overly-sensitive, sappy schmuck that you're now stuck living with...
*"Yes, I know I'm breaking your heart, but please don't make the mistake of thinking I care. Enough is enough—I've packed your stuff!"*

16. To that wretched reprobate who's got way too much stupid goin' on...

*"Your butt must get jealous of all the crap that comes out of your mouth! Holla!"*

17. Tell that two-timing cretin who took your low self-esteem to new and deeper depths...
*"You always bring me so much joy—whenever you leave the room. I'll get the door for you!"*

18. Let it be known to the lazy good-for-nothing loser who thinks you're his maid...
*"I am so done with you, it's beyond time for me to go! Don't bother to get upset—you wouldn't want to break a sweat!"*

19. Tell that wandering wuss who went from swoon-worthy to cringe-worthy...
*"I used to call you sweetheart, now I just want to fart on you."*

20. Announce to that miserable miscreant who always made you cry...
*"I gave. You took. I'm gone. Toodles!"*

For significant "she" jerks...

1. Break the news to that clingy, nagging, needy, nuisance of a girl...
*"I'm buying you a one-way ticket to get the hell away from me!"*

2. Make it known to the tacky Baby Mama minx that your mother warned you about...
*"Jesus might love you, but everyone else thinks you're a tramp. C-ya skeeza!"*

3. Tell that bootylicious girl named Daisy, who's got crazy she ain't even used...

*"We'll let bygones be bygones as soon as you be gone, OK? Now where did I put that can of "Witch-Be-Gone?"*

4. To the slutty seductress you couldn't resist sleeping with...
*"I'll never forget the first time we met. But I'll keep trying. Please leave now, as I have called the police to report a skank sighting, and they are in route."*

5. Invite that drop-dead gorgeous stalker girl to...
*"Come meet my last girlfriend. She's still chained up in my basement."*

Feel free to mix and match your type of significant jerk with the appropriate and most gratifying break-up line(s). All of the above may also include this one-line-fits-all-jerks as they exit: *"Don't let the doorknob hit you where the good Lord split you!"*

# Love Makes the World Go Round, But Laughter Keeps Us From Getting Dizzy

**Always February 8-14**

## Light Up and Hype Up Your Love Connection

As far as wild and wacky holiday-*ish* occasions go, *Love Makes the World Go Round, But Laughter Keeps Us from Getting Dizzy Week* gets my vote for having the wackiest title. Always the week leading up to Valentine's Day, and running parallel to *Dump Your Significant Jerk Week*, this special occasion was created to encourage people to seek out and celebrate the humor in our relationships. Its mission is to inspire us to "lighten up" our love connections and "hype up" the connection between our hearts and hearty laughter.

"Laughter is the best medicine" is not just for bumper stickers and memes. Multiple medical studies have proven that hearty laughter is like jogging for the heart. During the week of February 8-14, do your part to help strengthen your heart and your sweetheart's heart. Ideas for creating hearty laughter during *Love Makes the World Go Round, But Laughter Keeps Us from Getting Dizzy Week* include having a date night (or two) that involves doing something designed to make you LAUGH...

> *"I love you like a pig loves not being bacon!"*

- Take dance lessons for something fun like Polka, Line Dancing or Flamenco Dancing.

- Go to a Comedy Club.

- Spend an evening together at a gay bar *(they're way more fun than straight bars)*.

- Watch a couple of romantic comedies during the week, but make sure they're movies that both gals and guys will enjoy, like: *Crazy Stupid Love, When Harry Met Sally, Hitch, Date Night, Overboard, Friends With Benefits, Silver Linings Playbook, Think Like a Man.*

Make every day of this week special by whispering sweet nothings in your sweetheart's ear. Do this when they least expect it, like when they're changing the baby's diaper or taking out the trash, or when one of you is being yelled at for not taking out the trash or not changing the baby's diaper. Say something lovingly funny to him or her like...

- I love you with all my boobs. I would say heart, but my boobs are bigger.

- You're the nothing, my Darling, when people ask me what I'm thinking about.

- I love you more than I love beer, my Princess. And I reeeeally love beer!

- It looks like you're suffering from a lack of Vitamin Me.

- Do you have a band-aid, because I just scraped my knee falling in love with you.

- You're the cheese to my macaroni, baby!

- I don't know how you do it, Sugar, but you always make me laugh when I'm trying my best to be cranky.

- You remind me of bacon, my love—you make everything better.

- Marriage is a lot like the Army, Sweet Cakes. Everyone complains. But you'd be surprised at the large number that re-enlist!

- Knock, knock. Who's there? Olive. Olive who? Olive you.

- Yes, Pumpkin, I have a dirty mind. And right now, you're running naked through it.

- I love you so much, Sweet-ums, that even when I tell you to go to hell, I worry about you getting there safely.

- I love you like a pig loves not being bacon!

- Cute guys have always made me crazy. Hot guys always made me drool. Cool guys always made me daydream. And then came you, Cuddle-bear. You made me laugh, and I fell in love.

- I love you more than chocolate, Honey Bear. But please don't make me prove it!

- I love you so much, I'd fight a bear for you. Well, not a grizzly bear because they have claws. And not a panda bear because they know Kung Fu. But a Care Bear, I'd definitely fight a Care Bear for you!

- I will always love you, my handsome stud-muffin, no matter how fat I get.

Feel free to put your own creative spin on any of the above, and/or add your own personal nicknames. To make them even funnier, remember, it's all in the delivery. Like saying the "Olive you" line after stuffing your mouth full of olives. You'll know you've succeeded in giving your mate's heart a truly healthy workout when you hear them say, "You made me laugh so hard, tears ran down my leg!"

MAR

# MARCH
# Is International Mirth Month

Mirth is like the Viagra of good cheer!

## Mirth is Like the Viagra of Good Cheer!

As many of us go about our day-to-day lives, exercising our right to the pursuit of happiness, the stresses and pressures of daily life can often show us that life can sometimes ... suck! On life's most challenging days, when you feel you've got absolutely nothing to smile about, a little moment of mirth can actually go a long way in turning any frown upside down. "Mirth is like a flash of lightning that breaks through a gloom of clouds and glitters for a moment; cheerfulness keeps up a kind of daylight in the mind, and fills it with a steady and perpetual serenity." ~Joseph Addison

That insightful quote is from an English poet that most of us Yankees have never heard of, but we *have* heard that "Laughter is the best medicine!" According to a guy who calls himself Mr. Jollytologist, the best way to find humor in stressful situations—at least during the month of March—is for people all over the world to

> *Daily doses of mirth can erect a daily disposition of cheerful contentment.*

celebrate the month with mirth. And that's why he gave March a makeover and turned it into *International Mirth Month*!

Research studies have proven time and time again that we should never underestimate the mighty power of mirth. You see, mirth is like the Viagra of good cheer! Mirth makes it possible, it enhances it, and it makes it last longer. It's a cure for E.D.! Not for Erectile Dysfunction, but for other afflictions that can make one's life **E**motionally **D**ysfunctional ... **E**ternally **D**ismal ... **E**ndlessly **D**epressing. And just like that little blue pill, just one little moment of mirth can perk us right up when we're down in the dumps. Daily doses of mirth can erect a daily disposition of cheerful contentment. Side effects include: laughter, levity, and elation. And you don't have to seek immediate medical help, even for elation lasting more than 4 hours!

Celebrate *International Mirth Month,* using a creative and natural prescription by tapping into your inner pharmacy for 4 weeks of frequent mirth, designed to treat and cure whatever ails you better than any drug prescribed by a doctor.

Q: What are the two main ingredients in Viagra?
A: Miracle Gro & Fix-a-flat!

See! Didn't that mini moment of mirth lift your spirits just a tiny bit? But unless you're inclined to sit around and Google jokes all day *(which is totally not a bad thing),* it's not always easy to find many moments of mirth on any given day, especially stressful days. So, again I say, that's why that Mr. Jollytologist guy (aka Allen Klein at www.allenklein.com) came up with the idea for *International Mirth Month*!

Now whether this Jolly guy knew it or not, there's actually a multitude of mirthful days already in the month of March. Continue reading and you'll learn about happy holiday-*ish* occasions that were created by other like-minded and jolly people—days we can use and choose to celebrate, commemorate, or just plain contemplate. It must also be noted that these days have little to do with March Madness, because they're all about March Gladness!

# Let's Laugh Day

## Always March 19th

## LOL Can Be a Cure For Whatever Ails You

E very year on March 19th, people all over the country make the decision to get together, get happy and laugh their as*es off! *(I can say that, right?)* Why do they do this? Because in the words of the late, but still honorable Milton Berle, "Laughter is like an instant vacation!" And also because March 19th is *Let's Laugh Day.*

Many Internet websites list the day as *"National" Let's Laugh Day*, so feel free to acknowledge the day by spreading laughter from coast to coast on Facebook and/or other social media. And if it's not "national" in your area, feel free to acknowledge the day by spreading laughter from sea to shining sea on Facebook and/or other social media. *(Yes, I know that's redundant, I just wanted to make sure you're paying attention.)*

*Let's Laugh Day* encourages us to laugh, not so much for enjoyment, but so we can enjoy the health benefits of laughter. And as you'll see from the multitude of

---

*Some people "get high with a little help from their friends," and some people get high with a little help from "endorphins."*

---

times I'll be mentioning those benefits throughout this book (which is designed to make you laugh), multiple medical studies figured out long ago that "Laughter is God's Medicine," and they also identified an extensive list of laughter's benefits, including, but not limited to:

• Everyone feels better after experiencing a moment of mirth.

• Laughter helps us to relax, it diminishes pain, boosts our energy, eases anxiety and fear, strengthens our hearts and immune system. *(Wow, I feel better already.)*

- Laughing is like jogging for the heart, and 10-15 minutes of good, hearty laughter can easily burn up to 50 calories and improve our mood for up to several hours afterwards. *(Who the heck needs a treadmill when all I need is "Comedy Central")?*

- Laughter Therapy, also called Humor Therapy is being used more and more as a natural physiological treatment to help relieve physical and emotional stress and discomfort. *(That sounds a whole lot better than Shock Therapy, doesn't it?)*

- Laughing triggers the release of the body's natural feel-good chemicals, endorphins. *(Yeah. Some people "get high with a little help from their friends," and some people get high with a little help from "endorphins.")*

If you're still skeptical about the miraculous power of mirth? Check out these mirthful words of wisdom from noted authorities on the subject:

- "We don't laugh because we're happy—we're happy because we laugh." *~William James, aka "The father of American Psychology"*

- "Humor isn't for everyone. It's only for people who want to have fun, enjoy life, and feel alive." *~Anne Wilson Schaef, Author*

- "Laugh, and the world laughs with you. Laugh hysterically, for no apparent reason, and they'll leave you alone." *~Somebody on the Internet*

- "A day without laughter is a day wasted." *~Charlie Chaplin, famous funny man*

- "You don't stop laughing because you grow older. You grow older because you stop laughing." *~Maurice Chevalier, an old actor only old people remember*

- "Laughing together is as close as you can get to a hug without touching." *~Gina Barreca, feminist humorist*

- "I don't trust anyone who doesn't laugh." *~Maya Angelou, award-winning poet*

- "Laughter is the sound of the soul dancing. My soul probably looks like Fred Astaire." *~Jarod Kintz, humor and entertainment author*

If you're interested in paying tribute to *Let's Laugh Day*, (locally or nationally) here's some ideas:

- Add a laughing ringtone, app or video to your phone and play as needed, or post a laughing video on social media. Just hearing laughter primes our brain and puts smiles and chuckles on alert, and can even pull an LOL

  *Sign up for a "Laughter Yoga" class.*

  from the Sour Pusses and Grumpy Guses in our lives, not to mention the total strangers that you encounter when you play the sound during your subway ride to and/or from work.

- Send some LMAO *(laughing my a\*\* off)* memes to those you care about enough to want them to laugh til it hurts.

- Schedule a day of doing laugh-worthy activities like watching a sitcom marathon, play twister with the kids, visit a comedy club, watch a collection of YouTube's funniest animal videos.

- Sign up for a "laughter yoga" class. Can't find one in your area? Why not start one then?

- If you're daring, put the contagious component of laughter to the test. All you need is yourself and one other person to start laughing hysterically in a place where others can witness the interaction. Now see how many other people you can draw into your laugh gathering by doing nothing but laughing. Even faking it is supposed to have the ability to spread giggles, grins and chuckles galore!

# International Day of Happiness

Always March 20th

## The United Nations Wants Us All to Be Happy

*International Day of Happiness* is March 20th. Woo-hoo! It actually kicks off *Act Happy Week*. Together, that's seven whole days in a row when people are seriously expected to either *be* happy or *act* happy! *Seriously?* Yes, seriously. Our happiness is apparently of serious concern among the creators of *International Day of Happiness*. Who are these foolhardy peddlers of frivolity? Would you believe The United Nations?! *(Wait, what?)*

That's right, that international, inter-governmental organization that was created to promote international cooperation—The United Nations—wants you, us, the world, to be happy. Every year. On March 20th.

*International Day of Happiness* is a U.N. resolution that was adopted in 2012 by consensus of all 193 member countries. In other words, *IDOH* isn't just one of those wacky made-up fake holidays, this is the real deal! *IDOH* is celebrated around the world every March 20th as a day to recognize that happiness is a fundamental human goal, and calls upon countries to approach public policies in ways that improve the well-being of all peoples. The ultimate goal is to attain global happiness through economic development that is accompanied by social and environmental well-being. The U.N. provides educational tips, tools and seminars to educate countries and increase their awareness of the benefits of happiness. *(I wonder if the U.N. flies a Smiley Face flag for IDOH?)*

The whole idea of a day of happiness apparently came from a country in the Himalayan Kingdom. The citizens there are considered to be some of the happiest people in the world because of their holistic approach to life and the amount of importance they place on the well-being of the kingdom's people. That's certainly something other countries like ours could learn from. This kingdom of happy Himalayans measures its national and societal prosperity, not with a GNP (Gross National Product) like we do, but with a GNH—Gross National Happiness Index! *(Attention all Grumpy Guses of the world: Start packing, cause we've found you a new home!)*

> *These people are already living in a state of perpetual bliss. And it's by government decree!*

This is not a joke, people! These folks are totally serious about their happiness! They place just as much importance on the spiritual well-being of their citizens and communities as they place on economic and material wealth. Here we are in the good old U.S. of A., spending our days in the *pursuit* of happiness, when these people are already living in a state of perpetual bliss. And it's by government decree! That's like saying it's the law—you gotta be happy! (*Or what?*) Does that mean that if Grumpy Gus moves to their country and continues to be a sour puss, he could be deported?

For those of you who are perpetually unhappy enough to want to visit or even move to this happiness haven in the Himalayas, but don't quite remember where the region is, just turn right at Tibet. It might also be a good idea to practice your happy dance before your arrival, just in case auditions are required before you can become a citizen.

But for those of us who just wanna have a day of happiness, check out some of the IDOH activities on their website. (www.happinessday.org) for ideas, then share what you find with friends and family about how not to be grumpy, cranky, gloomy or unhappy on such a seriously happy day.

# Quirky Country Music Song Titles Day

## Always March 27th

### Top 40 Quirkiest Country Music Songs Titles of All Time

In keeping with March being *International Mirth Month* and all, a day like *Quirky Country Music Song Titles Day* fits right in with the other wild and wacky holiday-impersonating days in March. In fact, when I was writing *Let's Laugh Day* (always March 19th), I actually used a list of Quirky Country Music Song Titles as one of my primary sources for giggles and grins!

It doesn't matter if you're a fan of country music or not, and it doesn't matter that *Let's Laugh Day* has come and gone. This stuff is hilarious enough to turn any day into "Let's Laugh Ourselves Silly Day!" Here's one of my favorites: "I Got Tears In My Ears From Lying on My Back Cryin' Over You!"

See! That one's got LOL written all over it! Celebrate *Quirky Country Music Song Titles Day* this March 27th by sharing this version of the *Top 40 Quirky Country Music Song Titles*, past and present. See how many of these songs you and your friends and family can relate to, past or present. Or … have a contest to see who can come up with the funniest and quirkiest song titles for other music genres like Rock, Rap, Blues, Disco or Elevator music. Good luck coming up with stuff that's funnier and quirkier that these:

> *"I'm So Miserable Without You, It's Like Having You Here!"*

1. Get Your Tongue Outta My Mouth Cause I'm Kissing You Good-bye

2. How Can I Miss You If You Won't Go Away

3. You Done Tore Out My Heart and Stomped That Sucker Flat

4. My Wife Ran Off with My Best Friend and I sure Do Miss Him

5. I Still Miss You Baby, But My Aim's Getting Better

6. If the Phone Don't Ring, You'll Know It's Me

7. She Got the Ring and I Got the Finger

8. If I Had Shot You When I Wanted To, I'd Be Out by Now

9. You're the Hangnail in My Life, and I Can't Bite You Off

10. I Keep Forgettin' I Forgot About You

11. If You Leave Me, Can I Come Too?

12. I Bought the Boots That Just Walked Out On Me

13. When You Wrapped My Lunch in a Roadmap, I Knew You Meant Good-bye

14. I Don't Know Whether to Come Home or Go Crazy

15. I'm So Miserable Without You, It's Like Having You Here

16. The Next Time You Throw That Frying Pan, My Face Ain't Gonna Be There

17. If Whiskey Were a Woman, I'd be Married for Sure

18. He's Got a Way with Women, and He Just Got Away with Mine

19. Welcome to Dumpsville, Population Me

20. I Don't Know Whether to Kill Myself or Go Bowling

21. Our Love is Illegal Because Our Names Ain't the Same

22. I'll Get Over You as Soon As You Get Out From Under Him

23. I'm Just a Bug on the Windshield of Life

24. If I Had a Nose Full of Nickels, I'd Sneeze Them All Atchoo

25. If I Can't Be Number One in Your Life, Then Number Two on You

26. If you Don't Leave Me Alone, I'll Go and Find Someone Else Who Will

27. I Would Have Writ You a Letter, But I Couldn't Spell Yuck!

28. I'm Drinkin' Christmas Dinner, All Alone This Year

29. If Fingerprints Showed Up on Skin, Wonder Whose I'd Find on You

30. She's Actin' Single, so I'm Drinkin' Doubles

31. I Can't Love Your Body if Your Heart's Not in It

32. Ever Since I Said "I Do," There's a Lot of Things You Don't

33. Thank God and Greyhound She's Gone

34. You Were Only a Splinter as I Slid Down the Bannister of Life

35. I Ain't Never Gone to Bed with An Ugly Woman, But I Sure Woke Up With a Few

And just so you don't think all quirky Country Music songs are about love lost, here's a few true confessions of good country lovin':

36. I Fell in a Pile of You and Got Love All Over Me

37. If You Don't Believe I Love You, Just Ask My Wife

38. I Wish I were in Dixie Tonight, But She's Out of Town

39. I'll Marry You Tomorrow, But Let's Honeymoon Tonight

40. If My Nose Was Running Money, Honey, I'd Blow It All on You

Kinda makes you wanna grab your cowboy boots (or purchase some) and kick your heels up for some good ol' country line dancing! Don't know how to line dance? That's what YouTube is for! And don't forget your Stetson.

Now go forth and acknowledge *Quirky Country Music Song Titles Day* by trying not to be a bug on the windshield of somebody else's life!

# Walk On Your Wild Side Day

## Always April 12th

### Take Your Mild Side for a
### Walk on Your Wild Side

Have you ever wondered what it would be like to "walk on the wild side" even if it's just for a day? Well, apparently, someone else wondered the same thing, only they went so far as to actually create a *Walk on Your Wild Side Day!* It's April 12th—every year.

Let's face it, many of us were born to be mild-mannered people who exist only to draw inside the lines of our lives—we prefer to live safely in ... the color of beige. Then there are those of us who were born to be wild! These are the people who tend to paint their lives in very bold and vibrant colors. Their lives are very unrestrained, shameless ... *wild.*

---

*This April 12th, be free, be fearless, be about walking on <u>your</u> wild side! It's just for the day, so why not?*

---

*Walk on Your Wild Side Day* allows us to be both! Be beige on April 11th and 13th, but on April 12th, be free, be fearless, be about walking on *your* wild side! It's just for the day, so why not? I know this crazy day is only an imitation of a real holiday, but it's also about you being given an opportunity to become an imitation of a real wild person, so let's *do* this!

*Walk on Your Wild Side Day* encourages us—dares us—to celebrate the day by doing something crazy different! Something adventurous. Something totally outside your comfort zone. Something no one would ever expect you to *ever* do—embrace your inner wild streak! Pick a color that's totally not you (like a neon pink or green) and dye your hair that color! Accessorize the hair with an appropriately colored outfit— neon pink or green if you're bold enough. Black if your hair already says it all.

*(You know what? I gotta think about getting some buttons made up or something that people could wear on occasions like this. That way, others will know that you're acknowledging "Walk On Your Wild Side Day"*

*and they won't just think that "you done lost yo damn mind" showing up at work with neon purple hair!)*

*WOYWS Day* is also a day to shed at least one of your shoulda, woulda, couldas, and just *go for it,* regardless of anyone's criticism. Quit that job you hate and start your own business! Trade the minivan in for a motorcycle! If these sound a little too daring, then tone it down and just *Walk on Your Wild Side* with something a little less permanent. Buy your-

*Think about turning what would be an ordinary day into an extraordinary day of freedom and audacity.*

self some leather and see what it feels like to be a Biker Babe for a day! Go zip lining! Or take a quick trip to Las Vegas. Or go zip lining *in* Vegas, baby!

Whether your wild side is something a bit more tame, like not wearing a tie for the day, or not wearing a bra for the day, think about turning what would be an ordinary day into an extraordinary day of freedom and audacity. Get the band or singing group back together and go perform in the park or in the subway. Join a protest. Start a hip-hop class for senior citizens. Instead of wearing your usual t-shirt and jeans, wear a business suit. With a bow tie! If you normally have the personality of a kitten, here's your chance to become a tigress!

*Walk on Your Wild Side Day* was created to inspire us to pretty much be as wild as we want, so long as it's all legal and you can still get up the next morning and go to work. So go for it! Kick your mild side to the curb for the day and take a walk on *your* wild side!

\* \* \*

# Nothing Like A Dame Day

## Always April 17th

## There Is Nothing You Can Name
## That is Anything Like a Dame

April 17th is *Nothing Like a Dame Day!* And there's nothing more multifaceted than the name ... *Dame!* Starting in the 13th century, the name *Dame* was synonymous with "female ruler," and then in the 14th century, the term began to include "housewives." Fast forward to the 1950s and the term had expanded to something that encompassed all manner of females ranging from the sweet freckled-face "girl next door," to the ballsy, brassy, boa-wearing "women of the theatre," to the superstar "blonde bombshells" on the big screen. Dames, dames, dames! *There's Nothin' Like a Dame!*

And there's nobody who can describe a *Dame* better than a certain group of young sailors singing a song on a South Pacific beach during WWII, in one of the most beloved musicals of all time, *South Pacific*. It doesn't matter if you like musicals or not, the lyrics to the song "There's Nothing Like a Dame" are outlandishly funny, as a bunch of lonely, lovelorn soldiers reflect on having everything they need, except *Dames*. Check out these amusing excerpts...

> *There is absolutely nothing like the frame of a dame!*

*We've got sunlight on the sand,*
*We've got moonlight on the sea,*
*We've got mangoes and bananas*
*We can pick right off a tree,*
*We've got volleyball and ping-pong*
*And a lot of dandy games.*
*What ain't we got? We ain't got Dames!*

*We get packages from home,*
*We get movies, we get shows,*
*We get speeches from our skipper*
*And advice from Tokyo Rose,*
*We get letters doused with perfume,*
*We get dizzy from the smell.*
*What don't we got? You know darn well!*

*We have nothin' to put on*
*a clean white suit for,*
*What we need is what there*
*ain't no substitute for,*
*There is nothing like a dame,*
*nothing in the world,*
*There is nothing you can name*
*that is anything like a dame!*

*Nothing else is built the same,*
*nothing in the world*
*Has a soft and wavy frame,*
*like the silhouette of a dame*
*There is absolutely nothin' like*
*a frame of a dame!*

*So suppose a dame ain't bright,*
*or completely free from flaws,*
*Or as faithful as a bird dog,*
*or as kind as Santa Claus,*
*It's a waste of time to worry*
*over things that they have not,*
*Be thankful for the things they got!*

*There is nothing like a dame,*
*nothing in the world,*
*There is nothing you can name*
*that is anything like a dame!*

*There are no books like a dame*
*and nothin' looks like a dame.*
*There are no drinks like a dame,*
*and nothin' thinks like a dame,*
*Nothin' acts like a dame,*
*or attracts like a dame.*

*There ain't a thing that's wrong*
*with any man here*
*That can't be cured by pullin' him near*
*A girly, womanly, female, feminine dame!*

Share this song to start a conversation on social media. If you're looking to celebrate the occasion in a really big way, organize a *Nothing Like a Dame* theme party where everyone comes dressed like a dame, including the guys!

And if you happen to be a "girly, womanly, female, *feminist*" who can do without men who call you a "dame," check out the lyrics to another *South Pacific* song favorite, "I'm Gonna Wash That Man Right Outta My Hair!"

# National Talk Like Shakespeare Day

## Always April 23rd

## For Some, Talk Like Shakespeare Day Is Pretty Much Every Day!

April 23rd is *National Talk Like Shakespeare Day.* Most of us are already familiar with phrases associated with William Shakespeare's plays. You know, phrases like "To be or not to be." But what most of us are *unfamiliar* with are the many modern-day phrases that originated from Shakespearian plays. In fact, believe it or not, many of us actually talk like Shakespeare pretty much every day!

No, I'm not saying that we go around every day saying things like "What is upeth mine peeps," because that might cause a sane person to reply "And you're the laughing stock of the entire group of peeps." But guess what mine peeps? "Laughing stock" is an expression that is a direct descendant of one of William Shakespeare's plays! Which play? I don't know and, frankly,

*Old Bill Shakespeare was the reason I developed a very vigorous aversion to English Literature when I was in school. It was all Greek to me!*

I don't care. In fact, old Bill Shakespeare was the main reason I developed a very vigorous aversion to English Literature when I was in school. It was all Greek to me! And guess what? Shakespeare said that too! "It's Greek to me" was yet another line from old Bill's lingo.

So as you can see, even with those few examples, it's obvious that we be talkin' like Shakespeare all the time! I mean, people mutter, "it's all Greek to me" practically every time they have to click "I accept" for yet another online mile-long set of Terms and Conditions. The fine print on some of those legalese-loaded agreements can take a full 20 minutes—not to read—but just to scroll to the bottom of! To whomever decided that people need to agree to million-word Terms and Conditions before we can buy a toothbrush online, all I can say is, "Off with his head!" But wait—I remember that one! "Off with his head" was from Shakespeare's *Richard III!*

As for commemorating *Talk Like Shakespeare Day*, some people plan to spend the day adding "eth" to the end of words, and tossing other words like "tis," "twill," "thou," "thee" and "ye" into their casual conversations. And that's all fineth and cooleth, but technically speaking, methinks we would be talking like Shakespeare even if we spent the day telling knock-knock jokes! Yes, mine peeps, "Knock-knock, who's there?" began with old Billy Shakespeare. Woweth!

> *"Knock-knock, who's there?" began with old Billy Shakespeare. Woweth!*

So, in case you decide tis best to pay tribute to *Talk Like Shakespeare Day* by reciting Shakespearean expressions that have truly stood the test of time, it wouldn't be nearly as difficult as you might think because there are dozens of these expressions that you and I both use every day! Hither art a few thee might already be using...

- For goodness' sake
- Love is blind
- Good riddance!
- Play fast and loose
- Forever and a day
- Wild goose chase
- You can't have too much of a good thing!
- Laughing stock
- Heart of gold
- Bated breath
- Jealousy is the green-eyed monster
- Dead as a door nail

- Eaten me out of house and home
- Off with his head
- There's something rotten in the state of Denmark
- Fancy-free
- In my heart of hearts
- In my mind's eye
- It's Greek to me
- Pure as the driven snow
- As good luck would have it
- You've got to be cruel to be kind
- Wear my heart upon my sleeve
- Kill with kindness
- Neither a borrower nor a lender be
- Make your hair stand on end
- Set my teeth on edge
- There's method to my madness
- Woe is me
- Knock, knock. Who's there?

If you prefer to experience the day by actually *sounding* like Shakespeare, just go online and Google a Shakespeare Translator or go to www.TalkLikeShakespeare.org and have at it. Then combine some of your own customized Shakespearian lingo with some of the ones above, and have a contest with your family, friends or co-workers to see who can actually tell which of the expressions are the real descendants of ol' Bill.

Or ... commemorate the day with a few choice knock-knock jokes:

Knock, knock.
Who's there?
William Shakespeare.
William Shakespeare who?
William Shakespeare cans so they explode when you open them!

Knock, knock.
Who's there?
Mike.
Mike who?
Mike Ingdom for a horse!

Knock, knock.
Who's there?
Toby.
Toby who?
Toby or not to be! That is the question.

Toby talkin' like Shakespeare today, or not to be. Now *that* is the question!

# Eat What You Want Day!

## Always May 11th

### Eat, Drink & Be Merry on
### Eat What You Want Day!

*E*at What You Want Day is May 11th. This day of delight was created not just for the foodies of the world, but for the countless individuals looking to dump their diet for a day and eat their fill! Doesn't really matter which one you are—if you like to eat, this occasion can be a feast, and merrymaking is the special of the day.

On *Eat What You Want Day*, you get to celebrate food by eating what you want—the entire day! It's a day of decadence devoted to indulging in one's favorite foods. All. Day. Long. People everywhere justify honoring the day by eating what makes them happy as a reward for spending so many of the other 364 days of the year *not* eating what they want. They go off their diets and even off their rockers!

To commemorate the day, some people will enjoy the simple pleasure of dining on a simple bowl of cereal ... for breakfast, lunch, and dinner. Others experiment with their favorite foods—together. Like chocolate chip cookie crumbles in their mashed potatoes. (Yum!)

*Stop obsessing over your muffin top or your spreading hips and explore the idea of spreading avocado over the top of your blueberry muffin.*

Go ahead, pour some gravy over the top of your pancakes. For something healthier, try a mouth-watering spinach and banana sandwich. Stop obsessing over your muffin top or your spreading hips and explore the idea of spreading some avocado over the top of your chocolate chip muffin.

*Eat What You Want Day* is also about grabbing your buddies and besties and paying tribute to the day by paying a visit to the different eateries in your area, and trying something new like sushi, chicken & waffles, crème brulée, grits or even octopus. Having a Thanksgiving dinner is always a crowd favorite for the day. Or chow down on cuisine from another country like deep fried Mars Bars—a Scottish favorite. This is not

> *Bacon-wrapped Twinkies are sure to please all guys everywhere.*

a day to be shy. Get creative and be unafraid to try the strange and the exotic. Drizzle pineapple juice over prime rib and have a side of pistachio nuts! (Mmm, tasty.)

Mothers can celebrate *Eat What You Want Day* in conjunction with *Mother's Day*, by revisiting some of those pregnant-lady food cravings, like Doritos and whip cream sandwiches, or brownies with mustard. And if you're looking to really challenge your culinary yuck factor, try onions soaked in pickle juice with ... cherries on top.

For most men, celebrating the day can be made easy by just adding bacon to any of the aforementioned meals or snacks. Bacon-wrapped Twinkies are sure to please guys everywhere. Or, instead of gathering for a pub crawl, organize a grub crawl! You won't even have to worry about having a designated driver if you do the day up right, and you could easily end up with enough doggie bags to feed a family of 40. But above all, people, let's not forget, it's *Eat What You Want Day* not "Eat *ALL* You Want Day!"

*Chow!*

\* \* \*

# National Root Canal Appreciation Day

## Always May 11th

### Who Has the Nerve to Appreciate Root Canals?

There's nothing that can set one's teeth on edge, quite like hearing that you need to have a root canal! Many would rather fight tooth and nail to keep from having such an agonizing procedure. And now, believe it or not, there's actually a *National Root Canal Appreciation Day*. It's May 11th. Every May 11th. Seriously.

Years ago, root canals ranked right up there with having to go through the labor pains of child birth, or the torture of having one's hair pulled out, one strand at a time ... by ants. Now, *National Root Canal Appreciation Day* is an official periodontal proclamation created by a dentist to bring attention to the new realities of this tooth-saving procedure. But no matter how many millions of teeth are saved every year by root canals, and no matter how many smiles have been rescued from the terrors of a toothless grin, people still have little or no appreciation for the procedure.

*It's all about helping the much-maligned root canal procedure to get the respect it deserves without continuing to be the punch line of countless jokes.*

That's why a Madison, Wisconsin dentist, Dr. Chris Kammer, has been trying to change our way of thinking by educating us on how some dental treatments have progressed even beyond tolerable, and has advanced in many cases to an almost ... pleasant experience.

In 2005, this dentist even went so far as to perform a root canal at his city's baseball park, at home plate, and then apparently convinced 5,991 baseball fans to brush their teeth simultaneously, setting a new national record. He then created *National Root Canal Appreciation Day* to mark the occasion—a proclamation in recognition of dental specialists everywhere who help to keep us all smiling and chewing. It's all about helping the much-maligned root canal procedure to get the respect it deserves without continuing to be the punch line of countless jokes.

Many people simply contemplate this imitation of a celebration while others commemorate the day by purchasing a new toothbrush, stocking up on their supply of dental floss, and scheduling their next dental appointment. It's their way of taking precautions and

*Still, it's hard to believe that most people could ever really appreciate a root canal day. Because they'd lose their nerve!*

showing respect for the perpetual power of plaque. Still, it's hard to believe that most people could ever really appreciate a root canal day. Because they'd lose their nerve! *(Ba-Dum-Bum-Ching!)*

\* \* \*

# National Chicken Dance Day

## Always May 14th

### Strut Your Stuff on National Chicken Dance Day

Looking for a reason to strut your stuff? Then you're in luck, because May 14th is a day when folks from coast to coast plan to do just that as they celebrate *National Chicken Dance Day*! Always May 14th, and originally called "The Duck Dance," it appears someone may have laid an egg on this occasion because it was difficult to find an exact purpose for this daffy day. Nevertheless, people everywhere love the Chicken

Dance. In fact, a new World Record for the Longest Chicken Dance Line was established in Mandan, N.D. in 2010 at their annual Independence Day Parade and Street Festival. Their line covered 1.627 miles! Any participants who didn't know how to do the Chicken Dance were told to just "wing it!"

So, go ahead, don't be chicken! Celebrate the day with family or friends by pushing the furniture out of the way, kicking off your shoes and kicking up your heels. Ruffle your feathers and strut your stuff so everyone can see who rules your roost. *National Chicken Dance Day* is always a great day for people to practice the Chicken Dance for all the upcoming weddings, birthday parties, bat mitzvahs and family gatherings that will undoubtedly feature this party favorite for all ages.

> *Organize a Chicken Dance-Off in gym class or your exercise class.*

Consider organizing a Chicken Dance Challenge or Chicken Dance-Off in gym class or in your exercise class. Get funky with it and form a Chicken Dance Soul Train Line over at the student center or down at the senior center. I'd bet the farm that there's a lot of senior citizens out there who remember my favorite, the "Funky Chicken," and who'd be more than happy to show everyone how to do it!

This would also be a perfect day to brush up on the Electric Slide, Bunny Hop and Hokey-Pokey moves that you'll need to remember how to do for the next wedding you get invited to. Oh, and let's not forget the Macarena! *Hey Macarena!*

* * *

JUN

# National Old Maid's Day

Always June 4th

## Old Maid? Who You Callin' Old Maid?!

June 4th is *Old Maid's Day*. An objectionable title for an exceptional day. This almost-official national holiday began at the end of WWII when soldiers were returning home, looking to get married, have kids, and live the American dream they had fought so hard for. Dances and socials were held in cities all around the country to give the thousands of returning men a chance to meet and greet with the *millions* of women who had been impatiently waiting for their return.

Millions of females *longing* to become a wife, *yearning* to become a mother.

The stereotypical old maid back then was an old (over 30), lonely, frumpy, unattractive prude with 19 cats—she was both pitied and mocked. These days, *Old Maid's Day* brings recognition to the modern day "bachelorette," and she's far from frumpy! Aside from having her own reality TV show, she's typically a smart, sassy, savvy woman who has chosen to delay marriage and children to focus on her career, or to enjoy the freedom of being unattached while waiting for her perfect mate to appear. She's independent,

*Rejoice in the freedom and empowerment that you have to choose an active, purposeful, independent lifestyle that comes not from being unattractive, but from being unattached.*

self-sufficient and has an extensive social media network of friends. She can spend frivolously on clothes, shoes, tattoos and online dating, and she would probably have to be in her 80s and using a walker before anyone would dare call her an Old Maid to her face! If she has cats, it's certainly no more than eight.

So to all the single ladies—divorcées and widows of all ages included—celebrate *Old Maid's Day* this June 4th by getting out and getting noticed. Rejoice in the freedom and empowerment that you have to choose an active, purposeful, independent lifestyle that comes not from being unattractive, but from being unattached and not being someone's "old ball and chain."

For a really good time, put on your best I'm-free-to-do-what-I-want-when-I-want attitude, and get your groove in gear for an evening of fun. Resolve to stop continuing to delay all your life's dreams just because your Prince Charming has somehow taken a wrong turn in his quest to find you. Hey, he's a guy and they don't like to ask for directions, even when their internal GPS has them looking for love in all the wrong places.

Try not to spend this special day searching again for Mr. Charming, because life's too short to just let your own life—a life that could very well be a very enjoyable, gratifying and productive life—pass you buy. Remember, the best things in life don't have to revolve around being somebody's spouse, especially if you "settled" for someone who ended up being a louse.

*Remember, the best things in life don't have to revolve around being somebody's spouse, especially if you "settled" for someone who ended up being a louse.*

So, grab your gal pals for a rowdy evening of *Old Maid Card Games**, while eating *Old Maid Cake** and trading "worst date ever" stories. Mix up some Old *Maid Cocktails** and drink a toast in celebration of single women everywhere who possess a very special power—the power to create a different happily ever after—not as a lonely, desperate spinster cat lady, but as an "unclaimed treasure."

**Google 'em all and have a ball!*

\* \* \*

# The Festival of Popular Delusions Day

## Always June 5th

## All Delusions of Grandeur
## Must Cease and Desist on This Day

June 5th is the *Festival of Popular Delusions Day!* (*Say what?*) Yes, you read that correctly. There are, in fact, annual festivals in certain parts of the world that celebrate this day of delusions. Some events actually began back on June 5, 1945, as a celebration of D-Day which occurred on June 6, 1944.

D-Day was the day the Allied Forces (the good guys) launched a massive invasion against the Nazis (the bad guys) that turned the tides of World War II. No, the "D" does not stand for Delusions. In fact, the meaning of the "D" has long been a mystery. Anyways, up until D-Day, the Nazis had harbored delusions of grandeur that they would win the war and rule the Earth for a thousand years.

The *Festival of Popular Delusions Day* commemorates June 5th, the last day before D-Day. That was the last day that Adolph Hitler and his wicked army were able to maintain delusions of taking over the world, because the mighty Allied Forces arrived on the scene, 150,000 strong, to save the day by opening up 150,000 cans of *whoop-ass* all over them nasty Nazi bastards!

Hooray for the good guys! That makes this *Festival of Popular Delusions Day* sound like something worth celebrating! Modern day tributes to the day involve performing reality checks in regards to popular delusions held by contemporary society,

*It is a day to align our delusional beliefs with facts and reality.*

including those held by ourselves. It is a day to align our delusional beliefs with facts and reality.

Take this popular delusion, for instance: "If you make a wish before blowing out all the candles on your birthday cake in one breath, and then you don't tell anyone, your wish will come true." *(Wait, are you saying we have to stop believing in that?)* Yes, my friends, even though it's a delusion that has always brought hope and joy to millions! Even though tens of thousands of children and adults alike would be crushed if they were forced to acknowledge that they're never, ever gonna get a pony?!

Many delusions of grandeur can be good, motivating and uplifting figments of our imagination that we often use to boost the happiness factor in our lives. Like believing that an itchy palm means you're about to come into some money. *(Wow, I always thought that one had been scientifically proven to be true.)*

The good news is that this *Festival of Popular Delusions Day* is only for one 24-hour day. June 5th, every year, that's it. So, go ahead! How hard can it truly be to spend just one day acknowledging the folly of your personal delusions of grandeur and pipe dreams. Do it, if only to prove to everyone that you're still sane—because believing in the 5-second rule for dropped food is not something sane people believe ... or will admit to believing.

Even though some people often confuse delusions with superstitions and old wives' tales, that doesn't really matter because a delusion by any other name is still a delusion. Some popular delusions that folks may need to put into reality check this June 5th include, but are not limited to:

- Believing that finding a four-leaf clover will bring you good fortune. *(That's always been one of my favorites.)*

- Believing that 50 is the new 30! *(OK, I'll consider giving that one up, but only because I prefer to believe "60 is the new 30.")*

- Being convinced that you would be happier (for women) if you were rich, taller, prettier, had bigger boobs, had smaller feet. Happier (for men) if you were rich, taller, had less hair on your back, and had bigger ... feet. *(Short, ugly, hairy people everywhere should rise up on this day and dump those delusions! You'll be happier if you do.)*

- If I pray hard enough, God will make my horrible hangover go away. *(Yep, been there, done that. Jesus Christ may have turned water into wine, but you can pray til the cows jump over the moon, and God ain't gonna help you with that one because He still has that hang up about drunkenness and gluttony being a sin.)*

- If I hold my dreamcatcher in one hand and my rabbit's foot in the other and chant, "I believe, I believe" over and over, George Clooney will appear as my Knight in Shining Armor! And he'll still be single. *(Sure, that could happen.)*

*For the sake of reality, you must cease and desist with your fairy tale beliefs. But only on June 5th!*

- If you keep your fingers crossed, you won't get pregnant the first time. *(No, you silly girl, it's "if you keep your legs crossed, you won't get pregnant the first time!")*

- Happy wife, happy life! *(Hold up, wait a minute! That one is neither a delusion, superstition nor an old wives' tale! That one has been scientifically proven to be true!)*

- Still believing along with your kids that there really is a Santa Claus and a pot of gold at the end of the rainbow. *(Because once again, these are not things a sane person should admit to believing!)*

So remember, no matter how much happiness and high hopes your delusions may bring, no matter what psychological benefits the mental health professionals believe these gimmicks can provide, they're still just fallacies, still illusions, still a fool's paradise, and for the sake of reality, you must cease and desist with all your fairy tale beliefs.

But only on June 5th! After that, it's back to business as usual baby, because as everyone knows, looking at life through rose-colored glasses allows us to live and maintain a façade of happiness of the highest order, no matter what reality throws our way or how many lemons life squeezes in our faces. Whenever that happens, just remember that all you have to do is wish it away while pulling the lucky end of a wishbone while knocking on wood, because that will never fail to make it all better. *No fooling.*

# Stupid Guy Thing Day!

## Always June 22

### In Recognition of Those Bonehead Boys and Their Boundless Brain Farts!

June 22nd is *Stupid Guy Thing Day!* Wait, what? It's just the one day? How can *Stupid Guy Thing Day* be for just one day? Stupid Guy Things happen *every* day—heck, every minute! Stupid Guy Things happen to women, however, every millisecond! And sometimes that's just happening to one woman!

I'll bet it was *that* particular woman who came up with the idea for *Stupid Guy Thing Day*. Research on the subject shows that the purpose of the day declares that since women are always talking about Stupid

Guy Things, this is a day devoted to celebrating them! Women everywhere are encouraged to simply make a list of *Stupid Guy Things* (SGTs) and pass it on.

---

*But let's not spend the day boy bashing, or stupid-shaming those poor souls who don't even know when they're being stupid. Instead, let's celebrate their stupidity!*

---

Wow, if one woman was to combine the lists of even a handful of her girlfriends, that list could probably stretch to the moon and back ... a couple of times. Heck, my list of SGTs *(from before I met my awesome husband who never ever does anything stupid ... that I care to mention)* would have stretched at least to the next county! But let's not spend the day boy bashing, or stupid-shaming those poor souls who don't even know when they're being stupid. Instead, let's celebrate their stupidity!

And just to be clear, we wouldn't be acknowledging the notion that all men are stupid—we'd simply be acknowledging the notion that all men do stupid things. A lot! Meaning they do it way more than women! Everybody knows how some guys just excel at being stuck on stupid. So it should actually come as no surprise that we now have this special day set aside just so women everywhere can celebrate, commemorate, or just plain contemplate stupid guy things for an entire day.

And if you're a guy reading this *(first of all, thanks for buying my book),* and you think that a day devoted to women sitting around, listing and sharing and giggling about your SGTs sounds mean, then ... *(again, thanks for reading my book, I hope you become a fan)* ... then all I can say is "You need to man up, and take it like a man, Bro!" *Stupid Guy Thing Day* is just one day when women can have tons of fun by turning the tables on men for the *dozens* of *decades* of us women having to endure the endless stream of *Dumb Blonde Jokes* and *Yo Momma Jokes!*

So ladies, let's get down and get goofy with it and share with your friends, the best of the bonehead boys and their boundless brain farts! Here's a sampling of SGTs that I found on the Internet, so they must be true:

*Did you hear the one about the guy who went to the dentist to get his Bluetooth fixed?*

• When told that he would have to take a DNA test to see if he was the father of someone's child, a guy asked, "Why do women never have to take a DNA test to see if the baby is theirs?" Then after receiving confirmation that he was, in fact, the Baby Daddy to a set of twins, this muscle-bound, super-jock asked his Baby Mama, "Does it take 18 months for twins to be born or just 9?"

• Did you hear the one about the guy who finally stopped to ask for directions by inquiring, "Can you tell me how to get from Miami to Florida?"

• How about the guy who went to the dentist to get his Bluetooth fixed?

• One knucklehead guy tried to fill his car with water so he could drive in the car pool lane!

Other ideas for commemorating *Stupid Guy Thing Day* involve getting together with friends, both male and female, and watching movies like *Jackass* or *Dumb and Dumber*, while eating crazy stupid things that are designed to wreak stupid havoc on your health, like deep-fried, bacon-wrapped Twinkies with a 64 oz. Double Gulp soda as a chaser. But, hey, it's just for the one day, right, so how stupid can it be?

# Embrace Your Geekness Day

## Always July 13th

## Geeks are at the Peak of the Coolness Spectrum

Geeks are the new ... cool! That's right, folks, many of us have actually witnessed the amazing transformation of how the geeks of the world have gone from being individuals who, back in the day, were meek and a little creepy, to nowadays where it's uniquely cool to be a geek. In fact, geeks are darn near at the peak of the coolness spectrum.

But if you were to look way, waaay back in the day, to the early 1800s, you'd find where a geek was a carnival performer whose act involved things like biting the heads off live chickens. Distasteful to say the least.

---

*Because the kingdom of geeks is now led by people like Bill Gates, Mark Zuckerberg, and Iron Man, geeks have become the new jocks ... the new rock stars ... the new sexy!*

---

Fast forward to now and ask any typical 6-year-old what they want to be when they grow up and a typical answer might be "a geek!" Because the kingdom of geeks—aka geekdom—is now led by people like Bill Gates, Mark Zuckerberg, and Iron Man, geeks have become the new jocks ... the new rock stars ... the new sexy!

*Embrace Your Geekness Day* is celebrated worldwide every year on July 13th. It was conceived several years ago as a special day for geeks to celebrate and embrace their lifestyle. Said lifestyle usually involves guys and gals who are heavily into things like: gaming, comic books, spending endless hours visiting strange places on the internet, and dressing up as vampires or superheroes. Because of the popularity of social media and gaming these days, practically everyone is professing to be a device-savvy geek of some sort. Which means *Embrace Your Geekness Day* is ripe and ready to level up to something that could eventually morph into Embrace Your *Coolness* Day.

So cool are the geeks these days, people actually want geeks as friends, and not just for free IT support, because everybody knows you can get free IT support from any 3-year-old. People not only want geeks for friends, people want to date geeks, to marry geeks, give birth to geeks ... people want to *be* geeks. *Embrace Your Geekness Day* is a delightfully zany occasion when millions of people will profess their geekness with pride, if only for a day.

For those who are already card-carrying members of geekdom, this remarkable day presents you with the opportunity to become SuperGeek, with only a minimum risk of being called a SuperFreak! For those of you who have absolutely no desire to be geeky even for a day because you still think geeks are a little creepy, or because you have absolutely no

*For guys, having a geek's brain is almost like big boobs on a girl.*

evidence of anything even geeky-ish in your DNA, take a chance and acknowledge *Embrace Your Geekness Day* by stepping out of your comfort zone and by doing the next best thing ... embrace a geek!

For folks who want to join in on the fun, honor the occasion by flaunting your geekness, or better yet, use it to get your "flirt" on! Seriously. For guys, having a geek's brain is almost like big boobs on a girl. The truth is, even nerds and dorks have been able to gain a ton of cool points because people often confuse them with geeks. While all three are stereotypically depicted as socially awkward, unattractive, athletically challenged, eye-glass wearing people with cringe-worthy wardrobes, the differences between a geek, a nerd and a dork are noteworthy.

Technically, geeks are the techy ones because they're usually associated with being an enthusiast or an expert in a technological field or activity. Nerds have typically devoted their lives to intellectual or academic pursuits. Dorks, however, are the duds of the threesome. They do have the same wimpy-loser quality about them that the others have, and they all share

---

*Gather the family for a rousting game of Star Trek Monopoly or an evening of binge-watching all four of the "Revenge of the Nerds" movies.*

---

the fashion sense of a doorknob, but dorks fall short on the coolness scale because they lack the high IQ of the geeks and nerds. And without that IQ, dorks may be perceived as just ... boobs.

Feel free to pay tribute to *Embrace Your Geekness Day* by wearing something appropriate like a pocket protector, or put tape on your glasses, or wear a t-shirt with E=mc2 and an Albert Einstein wig and post it on social media. One popular t-shirt I've seen says "Talk nerdy to me." Or wear anything related to *Star Wars, Game of Thrones, Dr. Who* or your favorite superhero. Gather the family for a rousting game of *Star Trek Monopoly* followed by an evening of binge-watching the first season of *The Big Bang Theory* or all four of the *Revenge of the Nerds* movies.

For me, I plan to celebrate *Embrace Your Geekness Day* by visiting the local costume shop and buying all the stuff necessary to transform myself into my favorite superhero geek, Wonder Woman! That beautiful nerdy geek by day, who lives in a world of ordinary mortals, until she hears a cry for help, after which she spins around until most of her clothes fall off, leaving a sexy babelicious superhero with brains as big as her boobs!

And remember, geeks are cool because they rule. *The world!*

# Gorgeous Grandma Day

## Always July 23rd

### Gorgeous Grandmas are the Extraordinary Grandmas

To many people, all Grandmas are gorgeous. It's sort of like that "all babies are cute," and "all brides are beautiful" way of thinking. But on July 23rd, which is *Gorgeous Grandma Day*, countless people will be holding their Grannies in a slightly higher esteem than they normally do the other 364 days of the year, and they're planning to help make their Grandmother's day a very special one. *Gorgeous Grandma Day* was created to be an entire day devoted to acknowledging and celebrating those Grandmas who are far more than special because Gorgeous Grandmas are the extraordinary Grandmas!

In order to qualify as an extraordinarily Gorgeous Grandma on *Gorgeous Grandma Day*, one does *not* have to be a woman who lives and breathes to beautify herself by lathering her body daily in assorted anti-aging creams, balms and ointments. One does *not* have to have maintained a youthful figure so that one can still squeeze into a pair of skinny jeans and a crop top that shows off one's tramp stamp tattoo. *Gorgeous Grandma Day* is for those special Grammies who possess the following attributes:

*She exudes a love for life and she ain't afraid to show it!*

- She must believe that she has her whole life ahead of her, not behind her. *(Not very easy to do if your Nana is 92, but that would be part of what makes her so special.)*

- She wants to get the most out of every single day. *(Even if she can't always remember what day it is.)*

- She wants to thrive, not just survive. *(Like the beautiful flowers so many Grandmothers grow in their gardens.)*

- She cares a great deal about maintaining a healthy mind and body. *(My Big Mama likes to complete the New York Times crossword puzzle while she's on break between her line-dancing and kick-boxing classes.)*

- She refuses to remain static—she's open to learning, to new ideas, to new challenges, and to new experiences. *(Skydiving, anyone?)*

- She still possesses the energy and vitality that would make someone in their 20s or 30s seem like they're ... her age. *(Like the thousands of Gorgeous Grannies who run the annual Grandma's Marathon in Duluth, Minnesota every June.)*

- She exudes a love for life and she ain't afraid to show it! *(Always has been, and always will be the life of every party.)*

- Oh, and she must have at least one grandchild to qualify as a Gorgeous Grandma. *(The world record for the most grandkids is around 130 including great-grandkids, but I'll bet that beloved MeMaw loves every one of them equally, even if she can never remember the names of more than two of them.)*

> *On July 23rd, make sure you take some time to show your darling Mimsy what a wonderful impact she has made on your life.*

These extraordinarily Gorgeous Grandmas may be wrinkled and gray-haired, but their inner beauty always shines through. On July 23rd, make sure you take some time to show your darling Mimsy what a wonderful impact she has made on your life. Listen to her wisdom and listen to her stories, even if you've already heard them 933 times, and even if her stories get grander and more incredibly unbelievable every time you hear them. That's your sweet Grams, and that's why she's gorgeous.

Spend the day with your beloved Bubbie doing the things she likes to do. Join her in her Aqua Zumba class or at her weekly Pinochle game, or let her teach you how to play Pickleball. Bake some cookies together like you used to when you were a kid, or bake some cookies together because you never had a chance to do that when you were a kid. Then watch a movie like the *Princess Diaries* movies about a queen grandmother who has to teach her geeky teen granddaughter how to be a princess. For something a little more rowdy, try watching *Dirty Grandpa*!

If you *are* a Gorgeous Grandma *(like me)* and you know for a fact that your grandkids are totally clueless about *Gorgeous Grandma Day*, then there's only one thing you can do my fellow Grammies. During the first week of July, call, text or email each of your grandchildren and apologize for forgetting to wish them a *Happy Grandchildren's Day*—which is always the second Sunday in June—and then casually mention how you know they would never, *ever* forget to wish you a *Happy Gorgeous Grandma Day*!

Then when they claim they've never heard of such an occasion, that's when you remind them that that's what Google is for and also remind them that Grandmas are like Moms ... only with extra frosting. Then sit back, relax, and wait for all the outpourings of love to arrive.

*Happy Gorgeous Grandma Day!*

\* \* \*

# Tell an Old Joke Day

## Always July 24th

Jokes are Funny...
Old Jokes are Funnier...
Old Jokes about Getting Old are the Funniest!

In the words of the honorable Milton Berle (old comedian from the olden days), "Laughter is an instant vacation." Everyone feels better after an instantaneous moment of mirth. July 24th is *Tell an Old Joke Day*! Why not commemorate the occasion by sharing and spreading instantaneous moments of mirth to the people around you? Need some comedic material?

Look no further, because gathered here are oodles of old jokes and quotes about getting old—because those are, of course, the funniest—and this is by far some of the funniest stuff to ever come along.

Celebrate *Tell an Old Joke Day* by enjoying this group of gags, one-liners and tomfoolery, and telling them to anyone who'll listen, because these are sure to make 'em laugh. Heck, there's enough material here to provide you with an entire stand-up comedian routine. So go ahead, be the reason someone laughs today. Whether it be the people you're sandwiched between on the subway, or your co-workers, your Facebook fans, or the police officer who's giving you a speeding ticket, many of these jokes are sure to make 'em laugh ... out loud!

*Old is when you sit in a rocking chair and you can't get it started!*

~ ~ ~

"If you live to be one hundred, you've got it made. Very few people die past that age." ~George Burns

~ ~ ~

"He's at an age that whenever a pretty, young girl smiles at him, he immediately looks down to see what is unzipped." ~Elmer Pasta

~ ~ ~

"Try to accept each other for who you are, and don't point out the fact that the hair he's losing on his head is now growing out of his nose and his ears." ~Peg Bundy

~ ~ ~

"Even when you're old and frail, there is always a lot to be thankful for if you take the time to look. For example, I'm sitting here thinking how nice it is that wrinkles don't hurt." ~A Really Old Person

~ ~ ~

"Women shouldn't get a tattoo. That butterfly looks great on your breast when you're 20 or 30, but when you get to be 70, it stretches into a condor." ~Billy Elmer

~ ~ ~

"Wrinkled is not one of the things I wanted to be when I grew up!" ~A Baby Boomer

~ ~ ~

"I've learned that life is like a roll of toilet paper. The closer you get to the end, the faster it goes." ~Andy Rooney

~ ~ ~

"Old age ain't for wussies. The good news is, it don't last forever!" ~Somebody's Great-Granddaddy

~ ~ ~

"I'm at an age when my back goes out more than I do." ~Phyllis Diller

~ ~ ~

"Two old people sitting on a bench, one turns to the other and says 'My butt fell asleep.' The other says, 'Yep, I heard it snore a couple of times.'" ~Minions

~ ~ ~

"I stay away from natural foods. At my age, I need all the preservatives I can get." ~George Burns

~ ~ ~

There are 4 stages of senility: 1) You forget names, 2) you forget faces, 3) you forget to zip up, 4) you forget to zip down. ~I forgot

~ ~ ~

"You know you're getting older when a sexy babe catches your fancy and your pacemaker opens a nearby garage door." ~An old geezer

~ ~ ~

You know you've gotten old when . . .
• Your ears are hairier than your head.

- You can live without sex, but not without your reading glasses.
- Having sex in a twin-sized bed seems absurd.

~ ~ ~

"Three old guys are out walking. First one says: 'Windy, isn't it?'

Second one says: 'No, it's Thursday!'

Third one says: 'So am I. Let's go get a beer.'"

~ ~ ~

"Two elderly gentlemen were sitting on a bench under a tree when one turned to the other and said, 'Albert, I'm 83 years old now, and I'm just full of aches and pains. I know you're about my age. How do you feel?' Albert said, 'I feel just like a newborn baby. No hair, no teeth, and I think I just wet my pants.'"

~ ~ ~

Old is when...
- You remember when the Dead Sea was only sick.
- Trying to have sex is like trying to shoot pool with a rope.
- Pulling an "all nighter" means not getting up to go pee!
- You sit in a rocking chair and you can't get it started.
- Going bra-less pulls all the wrinkles out of your face.
- Your sweetie says, "Let's go upstairs and make love," and you answer, "Honey, I can't do both!"

~ ~ ~

An elderly couple had dinner at another couple's house, and after eating, the wives left the table and went into the kitchen. The two elderly gentlemen were talking, and one said, "Last night we went out to a new restaurant, and it was really great. I would recommend it very highly."

The other man said, "What is the name of the restaurant?"

The first man thought and thought and finally said, "What is the name of that flower you give to someone you love? You know ... the one that is red and has thorns."

"Do you mean a rose?"

"Yes," the man said. He turned toward the kitchen and yelled, "Rose, what's the name of that restaurant we went to last night?"

*Happy Tell an Old Joke Day!*

# Happiness Happens Day

## Always August 8th

Now and then, it's good to pause in our pursuit of happiness and **Just Be Happy!**

## Happiness Happens.
## So C'mon, Get Happy!

Not only is August 8th special because it's *Happiness Happens Day*, the entire month of August is special because it's *Happiness Happens Month*! Wow, that sounds like a whole lot of happiness happening, doesn't it? So if you've been struggling to get your hands on any kind of happiness, here's your chance.

As it happens, *Happiness Happens Day* and *Happiness Happens Month* were both conceived by the *Secret Society of Happy People*. They're the same secret society who created *Hunt for Happiness Week* which is in January. And as I mentioned back in January, you've probably never heard of the SSOHP, hence the word "secret" in their name, so don't forget, mum's the word. (Visit www.sohp.com if you're looking for a place where it's cool to be happy and check out the *31 Types of Happiness* the members of this secret society live by.)

*Happiness Happens Day* was originally named "Admit You're Happy Day." It was probably a good idea to change that name, though, because with so much negativity in the world, it's easy to believe that asking some people to admit they're happy is like asking them to admit they're rich, when they clearly aren't. It's also far easier to admit, even for a pessimist, that happiness is probably happening at any given moment ... somewhere on the planet.

*It encourages us to celebrate the expression of happiness, and to discourage even the thought of raining on someone's parade.*

*Happiness Happens Day*, however, inspires people to look within themselves and to recognize the happy moments that can usually be found in our daily lives. It encourages us to celebrate the expression of happiness, and to discourage even the thought of raining on someone's parade. Easier said than done? Not really. It's actually easier than you might think if you remember that happiness is not always one big thing—it's often a lot of little things put together. So c'mon, Get Happy!

To help get you started, below is a sampling of some of "the little things in life" that we often take for granted. Celebrate *Happiness Happens Day* by taking a look at your life and seeing how many little things you can string together that might inspire you to break into your happy dance! Feel free to borrow a few of these, and if you start to get a feeling of Déjà vu, it's only be-

*See how many little things you can string together that might inspire you to break into your happy dance!*

cause this list contains some of the same little happy things that you saw for *Hunt for Happiness Week* because some are so nice, I had to say 'em twice!

- You still have all your teeth.
- It's Summertime!
- Ice Cream.
- All your kids are out of diapers.
- You're having a good hair day.
- Netflix.
- Nobody in the family is currently in prison.
- Online shopping.
- You recently helped a little old lady.
- Beer.
- You didn't get stuck in traffic today.
- Saturdays.

- Everyone in the family is free of cavities and lice.
- Your team won.
- Chocolate.
- You love your job and/or your neighbors.
- You can't remember the last time you received a call from a telemarketer.
- Air conditioning.
- You found a seat on the subway today.
- You don't owe anybody money.
- Bacon.
- Your kitten/hamster/ferret video just went viral.
- Indoor plumbing.

See how easy it is to spot happiness happening in our daily lives? Did you notice also that it's not necessary to look to someone else to make us happy? Commemorate the day by recognizing and acknowledging the things that can bestow upon you, a happy-go-lucky day. Then spread that joy to those around you as you encourage them to look on the brighter side of life. Try something like using your favorite social media to see who can come up with the longest / biggest / funniest list of happies. Or just contemplate the occasion by drinking a toast to *Happiness Happens Day* with lemonade, because happy people naturally turn lemons into lemonade.

And remember: Every now and then, it's important to pause in our pursuit of happiness and take time to acknowledge some of the things in our lives that ... aren't making us unhappy!

*Face it, Happiness Happens! So, c'mon, get happy!*

✳ ✳ ✳

# Serendipity Day

## Always August 18th

## Serendipity: Is it Magic or is it Science?
## Or is it Magical Science?

August 18th is *Serendipity Day*. Sounds almost magical, doesn't it? Well, in some ways, it *is* like magic. Ask any romantic, and they'll tell you all sorts of fairy tales about fate and destiny and serendipitous moments that they've experienced. Like, "I got a speeding ticket on my way to divorce court and it was love at first sight between me and the cop who wrote the ticket—it was like magic." The best way the average person might describe Serendipity would probably be to call it a "happy accident" or a "silver lining." But there are those who simply call it "magic."

*Even some scientists are convinced that Serendipity somehow involves science.*

On the other hand, if you're a realist—because you like to "keep it real"—then you are probably of the mindset that Serendipity is really just a whole lot of silliness dipped in a whole heap of hooey. But believe it or not, even some scientists, who tend to keep it real 24/7, are convinced that Serendipity somehow involves science.

Take the case of Silly Putty, for instance. It was invented totally by accident when an engineer was trying to create a new synthetic rubber for truck tires and soldiers' boots during WWII. It ended up being a total flop in that respect, but it also ended up being one of the most popular toys of the 20th century.

So if you look at it that way, well yeah, Serendipity can be real, even in the world of science. But what most of us don't know, is that in the scientific community, it is a known and respected fact that Serendipity has been a common occurrence throughout the history of scientific innovation.

Need more proof? Notta problem. There's plenty of proof of serendipity's magical and scientific powers all around us, if we just take the time to look. The creator of *Serendipity Day* encourages us to have "the willingness to live our lives as though everything is a miracle, and the belief that at any moment, something wonderful is about to happen." Sounds like somebody's trying to sell us fairy dust to sprinkle over our magic beans, doesn't it? But for just one day, August 18th, on *Serendipity Day*, why not play along?

To acknowledge the occasion, all you have to do is spend the day with a keen willingness to seek and share samples and symbols of Serendipity with others who might be looking to do the same. Like you friends, after you give them a heads up about August 18th being *Serendipity Day*. Make an effort to look for and notice all the unexpected good things that actually happen all the time—they're always out there if you have the eyes to see them. Some of you will see magical moments and some will see weird science, and some will see ... magical science. Here's a sampling of the many faces of Serendipity.

> *Serendipity is when you're looking for the perfect mate, but you find the imperfect one who is perfect for you.*

Serendipity...

- Is being in the right place at the right time.

- Occurred when a Scottish bacteriologist discovered penicillin from a moldy petri dish that he was about to throw away.

- Is when you're looking for the perfect mate, but you find the imperfect one who is perfect for you.

- Is like when Marilyn Monroe was discovered while working in a munitions plant during WWII.

- Is kismet!

- Happened when the Microwave Oven was invented as the result of an odd observation during a science experiment.

- Is when what you thought was a coincidence turns into something really awesome.

- Was the reason Chocolate Chip Cookies became the result of a dessert recipe gone wrong.

- Is in knowing that what is meant to be will always find its way.

- Is a fortunate happenstance.

- Was present when a customer in a restaurant kept sending back her "thick" fried potatoes, which caused the chef's patience to run so thin that he created what came to be known as potato chips!

- Is fate.

- Happened when Charlize Theron, the actress, was discovered while throwing a temper tantrum at a bank.

- Is when once in a lifetime happens twice.

- Is divine decree.

- Was the inspiration for a great quote: "When love feels like magic, it's called destiny. When destiny has a sense of humor, it's called serendipity." *~Serendipity, The Movie.*

So as you can see, Serendipity is ... like magical science at its best. "I was as surprised as anyone when my research on a potential treatment for heart disease revealed a side effect that sparked a sexual health revolution." *~The Doctor who discovered Viagra!*

\* \* \*

# Go Topless Day

## Always the Sunday
## Closest to August 26th

### Go Topless Day? You're Joking, Right?

August 26th is *Go Topless Day!* This is not a joke, my friends, this is a very real and annual event. They say you can't make this stuff up, but the truth is, somebody actually makes this stuff up! So you gotta wonder what kind of person would conceive of, and then promote such a wacky, *fake* holiday as this ... this ... "Bare-the-Boobies Day!?"

My guess is that it was someone who either has a real nice set of boobies, or it was someone who is a man. And if it turns out it was a man with a real nice set of boobies, all I can say is ... we should try not to stare. If it turns out it's just a man who's a boob, I say we chase him down and then make him the poster boy for a new and better—although still a *phony*—holiday that us ladies will make up. We could call it "Men Are Boobs Day."

*Go Topless Day should never, ever be celebrated or commemorated unless it is done simultaneously with "Men are Boobs Day!"*

And to prove the point that some or many or most (take your pick) men *are* boobs, and that there's a 99.9% chance *all* men would become boobs on *Go Topless Day*, let's put the men to the test. On August 26th, a bunch of us girls should gather together out in public, strip off our tops, and parade "Our Girls" for all to see. Then count the minutes it takes before dozens of Man Boobs of all ages begin to materialize out of thin air, all making a spectacle of themselves.

I figure it should take no longer than 5 minutes before guys from all walks of life start to emerge, camera phones in hand, mouths gapping, as many of them appear to be mouthing the words—thinking the words—saying the words—yelling the words: *Wow, look at all the Boobies!* Or, *Hey, get a load of those Jugs! Melons! Twin Peaks! Golden Globes! Chubby Chest Cheeks!* And don't be surprised, ladies, if you see a guy staring directly at you, all wide-eyed and trance-like, chanting, *I'm a boob for Bazookas* ... and you realize it's the town mayor. *OMG!*

So there you have it! That, my friends, is the reality of what a *Go Topless Day* event could entail. Ergo, *Go Topless Day* should never, ever be celebrated or commemorated ... unless it is done simultaneously with "Men are Boobs Day!" Fair is fair, and until both those days are treated equally as "official" fake holidays, *Go Topless Day* can only be classified as an official *joke!* Here's an example of why I say that. Question: What does a 75-year-old woman have between her breasts that a 25-year-old does not? Answer: A navel! See, it's a joke, people! A joke that conjures up a visual of my 75-year-old Nana—topless!

> *Question: What does a 75-year-old woman have between her breasts that a 25-year-old does not?*
> *Answer: A navel!*

And even if I, personally, had the knockers of a 25-year-old, there's no way I'd want to parade myself around in public with my bosom bouncing around all over the place! Therefore, *Go Topless Day* is going to be one of those counterfeit holidays that my Nana and I do not plan to celebrate or commemorate, but we've got some serious contemplating going on about this ... this ... "Epic Boobage Day!"

You know what else is a joke? The *purpose* of *Go Topless Day* which is "Free Your Breasts! Free Your Mind!" Interesting concept, to say the least. And believe it or not, both the concept and the fabricated holiday were conceived by a spiritual leader. (*Wait, what?*) Said spiritual leader feels that women have the same constitutional right that men have to go bare-chested in public. He or she goes on to say, "As long as men are allowed to be topless in public, women should have the same constitutional right. Or else, men should have to wear something to hide their chests."

Anyway, this spiritual leader person has started an entire movement, which includes the celebration of *Go Topless Day* every year, always on the closest Sunday to *Women's Equality Day* which is always August 26th. *Women's Equality Day* is in recognition of the happy day in 1920 when women were granted the right to vote on the basis of gender equality. Now, all these years later, gender equality is again the basis behind this movement for a woman's right to ... to ... air her ta-tas in public!

Regardless of the countless men who will go coo-coo for the ta-tas on *Go Topless Day*, if you're a woman who wants to be loyal and supportive of the growing movement for things like equal pay, then go for it! With such a noble cause as its foundation, that sort of makes *Go Topless Day* seem rather empowering and ... uplifting. Kinda makes you wanna jump up, paint "The Twins" in the stars and stripes and run a couple of laps around the block with an American Flag tied around

*We ladies already know that most men are card-carrying members of the "Boobs for Boobage Club."*

your waist, as you wave a sign that says "Equal Topless Rights for All!" You could even carry a sign that says "Honk if you like Hooters" but unfortunately, it won't matter one bit what the signs say, because ain't nobody gonna be lookin' at any signage with all that magnificent bouncing boobage to see!

To the men reading this, believe it or not, there's no need for you to feel offended by any of the aforementioned paragraphs because there's no harm intended. You see, we ladies already know that most men are card-carrying members of the "Boobs for Boobage Club." We also know that it really doesn't matter what shapes or sizes or colors our bosoms are, our men can almost always be depended upon to ogle them as often as they can get away with. *(Yeah, we see you seeing us.)* Most importantly, however, we also know how much our men adore our bosoms, and cherish them and love them, sometimes even more than we, ourselves, do. And when it's the right guy doin' all those things, that's some of what we women adore and cherish and love most about you!

*Go Topless Day events are planned every year in over 60 cities around the globe, including Go Topless Pride Parades in states like New York and California.*

So ladies! If you've got the insane type of courage it takes to stand up for Women's Equality by stopping traffic with your ... traffic stoppers, I say go for it! For details on how to join in on the celebrations of *Go Topless Day* (or protests depending on your local laws), just Google the topic or visit the official website (but parental discretion is definitely advised when visiting www.GoTopless.org). Events are planned every year in over 60 cities around the globe, including *Go Topless Pride Parades* in states like New York and California.

Show your support for a woman's right to be topless wherever a man can be topless, whether it be in your own back yard or in a parade down Main Street. Carry signs like "Women's Breasts are Family Friendly." All male participants are encouraged to wear bikini tops to symbolize how unfair the laws are and how uncomfortable bras are. They can carry signs saying things like "Free Your Nipples, Free Your Mind!"

My spunky old Nana is so excited about celebrating *Go Topless Day* that she's actually planning to show up topless at her job down at the Senior Center to protest the lack of equal pay there. She's more than a little nervous, though, because she teaches senior kick boxing there and she's afraid that teaching while topless will make her hooters start high-fiving everyone!

High five to *Go Topless Day!*

# The Anniversary of the Prohibition of ... Toasts?!

## Always September 4th

## Cheers to the Day Politicians Proposed
## The Prohibition of Proposing a Toast!

September 4th is a day that *should* be commemorated every year based solely on the absurdity of what happened on that day nearly 380 years ago. For September 4, 1639 was the historically baffling day when a group of politicians in the state of Massachusetts got together on what was apparently a very lackadaisical legislative session and decided to waste the taxpayers' money by passing a ludicrous law that prohibited the practice of *drinking toasts*!

I'm not talking about the practice of sipping on a refreshing glass of toasted bread, because banning that would be slightly less ludicrous. No, this group of public servants literally made it illegal to propose a toast! In other words, raising your glass of ale to someone, and saying "Cheers!" was somehow a threat to ... what? National security? Seriously?

---

*The Colony's Founding Fathers, being mostly Puritans, sought to "purify" its population by prohibiting any type of inappropriate merriment.*

---

This first official alcohol-related prohibition in the New World was enacted shortly after Boston's first Brew Pub was opened. The Colony's Founding Fathers, being mostly Puritans, sought to "purify" its population by prohibiting any type of inappropriate merriment. Oddly enough, the Puritans approved of the moderate consumption of alcohol, but their lawmakers considered the common custom of drinking to one another's health, happiness or holidays, to be a useless ceremony. So they made it illegal.

That all changed six years later in 1645—the happy day in history when the authorities repealed the law. They had finally found it futile to fixate on finding fault with all the footloose and fancy-free, toast-proposing citizens who had already concluded that these lawmakers were full of it! Much like the 18th Amendment of the Constitution—also known as the Great Prohibition—which was a national experiment that took away the inherent right of Americans to booze it up, both of these "noble" experiments were epic failures.

The Great Prohibition period of 1920-1933 became an infamous era in American history when the entire nation seemed to flip the bird at the Federal government. Bootlegging gangsters ruled the roost, Speakeasies became very plentiful and very prosperous, and it became very fashionable to break the law. So instead of Prohibition encouraging our nation to value a society of people with minds and bodies free from the undermining effects of alcohol, prohibiting liquor inadvertently made drinkers of nearly everyone!

*Lift your latte to the bus driver or Uber driver and proclaim, "Mazel tov!"*

At this juncture, I would like to propose a few suggestions for suitable ways to pay tribute to the preposterous day so long ago on September 4th, when toasting became toast. We, being citizens of the 21st century, where many of us are enjoying the intoxicating effects of entitlements, I say we celebrate this inauspicious occasion by making it fashionable to break the law of 1639 this September 4th. I propose that we honor the day by exercising our inherent right to propose a toast to whomever we please, whenever we please, wherever we please, and with whatever we damn well please! And ain't no politician gonna tell us that we can't!

Here's some simple, easy and effortless ways that you can exercise your right to be the "Toast of the Town." Be sure to share these with your friends and family so they can join in on the fun, as well. People will have no idea what you guys are doing, but I can almost guarantee there will be smiles.

- Lift your latte to the bus driver or Uber driver and proclaim, "Mazel tov!"

- Raise your cappuccino towards the cop directing traffic and propose, "May you always have love, laughter and happily ever after."

*Hoist your baby's bottle of milk into the air and announce, "Here's lookin' at you, kid!"*

- Hoist your baby's bottle of milk into the air and announce, "Here's lookin' at you, kid!"

- Offer a smoothie to your mail carrier as you propose, "May the neighbors respect you, trouble neglect you, angels protect you, and heaven accept you."

- To your newlywed neighbors: "May 'for better or worse,' be far better than worse."

- Over after-school cookies and milk with your kids: "Over the lip, through the gums, look out gut, here it comes!"

- Raise your martini to your mate and declare, "May our home always be too small to hold all our friends ... and also too small for relatives to move in."

- Clink bottlenecks with your friends and proclaim, "Beer is proof that God loves us and wants us to be happy."

- At the company-sponsored dinner event: "To all the fine people who came out tonight, and to all the people I work with, too ... Cheers!"

- At the monthly meeting of the Cheaters Club: "Here's to our wives and girlfriends, may they never meet."

- To the local barkeep:
  "Of all my favorite things to do,
  The utmost is to have a brew.

  My love grows for my foamy friend,
  With each thirst-quenching elbow bend.

  Beer's so frothy, smooth and cold,
  It's like paradise—pure liquid gold.

  Yes, beer means many things to me...
  But that's all for now cause I gotta pee!"

*Cheers!*

# Wonderful Weirdos Day

Always September 9th

## Weirdos Can Be Wonderful If Only for a Day

September 9th is *Wonderful Weirdos Day*. "Normality is a paved road, it's comfortable to walk on. But no flowers grow on it." ~Vincent van Gogh

That was a very dignified way of saying how mind-numbingly boring normal people can often be. That said, if you consider yourself normal 24/7, then read no further because there's no need for you to bother to join in on the fun that can be had this September 9th on *Wonderful Weirdos Day*. On the other hand, if you're reading this book—a book about weird and wacky fake holidays—then you're probably weird enough in your own right to at least be intrigued by the idea of a *Wonderful Weirdos Day,* so I invite you to read on. At the very least, you can con-

*For those of us who have the ability to wear weird well ... well, we're gonna have some fun on Wonderful Weirdos Day because we're the weird ones who OWN it!*

sider this news you can use to amuse others, via whatever electronic venue you chose to amuse others.

For those of us who have the ability to wear weird well ... well, we're gonna have some fun on *Wonderful Weirdos Day* because we're the weird ones who OWN it! We work at it, we take pride in it, and we think it's both cool and wonderful to be weird. No doubt it was one of us weirdos who created this wacky impersonation of a holiday.

According to Chase's Calendar of Events (*The Godfather of Event Calendars*) *Wonderful Weirdos Day* is an occasion to acknowledge that, "All of us are blessed with one or two wonderful weirdos in our lives. These are the folks who remind us to think outside the box and to be a little more true to ourselves. Today is the day to thank them, so give them a hug, and say 'I love you, you weirdo!'"

Think about your weirdo brother or sister, or that weirdo aunt who belches the Stars-Spangled Banner for you every time she comes to visit. I've got a wonderfully weird 22-year-old grandson who thinks he's a vampire. Think about that weirdo biology teacher who dresses like a 1970s pimp, or that traffic court judge you saw that was dressed like a clown. How about that weirdo toll-booth dude with the Donald Trump neck tattoo who's always singing show tunes at the top of his lungs! These—often loveable characters—are the inspiration behind *Wonderful Weirdos Day*.

So what about you? What kind of inspiration would you need in order to feel the need to acknowledge *Wonderful Weirdos Day* in some way? Go ahead, try switching the gears on that creative side of your brain and kick it into overdrive to see how much fun you can have with this concept. Weird hats are easy to pull off, so wear a chef's hat or a 10-gallon hat at work.

---

*Throw a wonderful weirdo theme party involving a contest to crown the one with the most wonderful display of weirdness.*

---

Or take a cue from some of the aforementioned weirdos and start up a show tunes sing-a-long on the bus on in the line at the grocery store—you'll be surprised at how many people will join in. Show up at school with a weird, fake neck tattoo of Donald Trump, the orange version.

For those of you who wake up every morning to a cup of weird with a teaspoon of creepy, you certainly don't need any ideas from me on how to act like a weirdo. You're the kind that will show up at work on *Wonderful Weirdos Day* dressed as a Zombie. A true-blue weirdo would probably celebrate the occasion by getting a real tattoo of Donald Trump in their armpit. Now, *that's* creepy!

Also, nothing beats a gathering of friends like a theme party. Throw a wonderful weirdo theme party involving a contest to crown the one with the most wonderful display of weirdness. Encourage people to wear something weird, do something weird, or share something weird. You could even have weird prizes like a Zombie Survival Kit or a UFO Detector.

Being a weirdo can, indeed, be wonderful fun, and not just on *Wonderful Weirdos Day*. In fact, there are wonderfully weird days in every single month that you can celebrate, commemorate, or just plain contemplate. Here's just a few...

- Jan – National Run It Up the Flagpole and See If Anyone Salutes It Day
- Feb – Wave ALL Your Fingers at Your Neighbor Day
- Mar – Alien Abduction Day
- Apr – St. Stupid Day
- May – World Naked Gardening Day
- Jun – World Bike Naked Day
- Jul – Be Nice to New Jersey Week
- Aug – World Middle Finger Day
- Sep – Race Your Mouse Around the Icons Day
- Oct – Getting the World to Beat A Path to Your Door Week
- Nov – Practice Being Psychic Day
- Dec – Answer the Phone Like Buddy the Elf Day

This September 9th, dare to be different. Dare to be peculiar. Dare to be eccentric, or kooky or extraordinarily goofy. Dare to show how wonderful weirdos can be!

# Talk Like a Pirate Day

## Always September 19th

**Ahoy, Me Lily-Livered Landlubbers!**

Ahoy, Me Maties! September 19th is *Talk Like a Pirate Day*, one of the most celebrated and familiar fake holiday-*ish* days of the year! It's easy to join in on the fun, and you'll probably notice others throughout the day who will be doing their best to talk like a pirate, by tossing lots of "Arrrr's" into their otherwise normal conversations at work, on Facebook, on Twitter, on Instagram, on Snapchat, on YouTube, on Pinterest, etc., etc., etcetera!

But with sooooooo many social media outlets to try and keep up with, who has time to learn how to talk like a pirate? Do you? I didn't think so. Notta problem, I'm happy to help so here's a few suggestions that are sure to make everyone you encounter think that you're either a swashbucklin' pirate o' th' sea ... or that you're drunk.

You can start by letting everyone know that your pirate name for the day is something like *Black Bart, Blackbeard, Long John Silver* or *Cap'n Slappy*. Feel free to take things a step further by dressing like a pirate. Wear an eye patch or a pirate hat with skull & crossbones. If you decide to go even further and buy an entire pirate's costume, do try to remember to be frugal with your festivities and use the costume again for Halloween and/or your kid's next birthday party. Or keep it simple and just borrow your son's plastic sword and pin your daughter's stuffed parrot to your shirt, and a pirate you'll be! Then, spend the day scowling and being insulting, and adding words like "Me Hearties" to the end of sentences. Other pirate ideas:

*Pirate greeting:
Ahoy me scurvy
scallywags!*

Pirate greetings...
- Ahoy there matey!
- Ahoy me hearties!
- Ahoy me scurvy scallywags!

Pirate insults...
- What are ye lookin' at ye lily-livered landlubber!

- Aye, ye better do what yer told or ye be walkin' the plank ye pox-ridden flounder!

Pirate parenting...

- Here's yer dinner, ya mangy cockroaches!

Pirate invitation...
- Yer all invited to join me later for a Yo Ho Ho and a bottle of rum!

Pirate astonishment...

- Well shiver me timbers and blow me down, me wooden leg has termites!
- Thar she blows, me maties! The biggest booty any of us scallywags will ever see!

*Argh me maties! Now get back t' yer poop deck ye ole hornswaggler!*

Oct

# Silly Sayings Day

## Always October 13th

### In Celebration of the Silliness of Silly Sayings

Have you ever wondered about some of the silly sayings you often hear articulated by people like your grandmother? Silly sayings like, "Your Gramps is just the 'Bee's Knees!" Or how about when you hear your nutty-as-a-fruitcake neighbor—the one who walks her cat on a leash—announce to the cat "We're gonna 'Paint the Town Red' today, Mr. Wiggles!" Well, it's expressions like that, that probably prompted someone to propose that October 13th always be proclaimed as *Silly Sayings Day*!

To help those of us who wish to pay tribute to the occasion, let's explore a few popular silly sayings, along with their alleged origins. There are actually numerous versions of said origins, and selecting the best one was not easy so I used a method with a proven track record for accuracy ... any many miny mo!

*The origin of the expression "Skeletons in the Closet" apparently stems from the 1800s when physicians found it very difficult to acquire dead bodies in order to study them.*

Since October is the most popular month for freaky and creepy, let's start with the expression "Skeletons in the Closet." Almost everyone has a skeleton or two (or a few) in their closet. *(And for you young people, this expression has absolutely nothing to do with the multitudes of weird skull-adorned apparel you currently have in your closet.)*

Truth be told, pretty much anyone over the age of 30 (or anyone who ever went away to college) has some sort of deep, dark secret that they're ashamed of or embarrassed about. Something you wouldn't want your friends or co-workers, or social media to find out about. It could be a personal secret *(What the hell was I thinking!?)* or it could be a family indiscretion that's shrouded in secrecy *(Grandpa Leroy keeps getting arrested for growing pot in his basement.)*

The origin of the expression "Skeletons in the Closet" apparently stems from the 1800s when physicians found it very difficult to acquire dead bodies in order to study them. Remember how hard it was for Dr. Frankenstein to get his hands on cadavers? He solved his problems by robbing graveyards and morgues. That's not to say that's what *real* doctors did back then, I'm just saying that if a doctor were successful in somehow acquiring the skeletal remains of a deceased individual, he not only treasured it, he cherished it because it was such a valuable resource for research.

Society, however, and patients in particular, frowned on doctors who put their dearly departed on display, so the doctors would routinely stuff their stiffs in a closet. Over time, it was assumed that most physicians had such skeletons in their closets, hidden from general public knowledge. How many skeletons are there in *your* closet?

*"Don't throw the baby out with the bath water!"*

Our next silly saying is: "Don't throw the baby out with the bath water!" If you think that saying is more frightful than silly, wait til you hear about its origin. Spoiler alert: it's going to be shockingly foul! Today, however, the expression involves being careful not to discard something good while attempting to get rid of something bad that is connected to the good. Example: Don't kick your rich, handsome, and totally awesome boyfriend to the curb just because his feet smell so vile that you get *stank face* whenever he takes his shoes off! Don't dump the dude, just buy some Odor Eaters and Fabreeze and call it a day!

"Don't throw the baby out with the bath water" has one reported origin from several centuries ago, when it is said that people generally didn't bathe more than once every few months—some only once a year. *(Wow, that had to ignite some epic stank faces!)* And then when they did finally take baths, the whole family would use the same tubful of water! *(I warned you it was gonna be "shockingly foul.")* Legend has it that the man of the house bathed first, then the males, then females, then last (and apparently least), the babies. So when it came time to empty the thick, cloudy, smelly, scum-filled tub, extra care always had to be taken to make sure they didn't throw the baby out with the bathwater. *(OMG, I think I need a shower after that one!)*

Up next, let's examine the saying, "Hell on wheels." Modern day meanings for the expression often have to do with someone who is tough, hardcore, wild, extremely difficult and/or hard to handle. Example: Picture an angry, scorned ex-wife who is hell-bent on crashing her old beat-up car into her ex-husband's new convertible sports car after she spots him driving in the next lane with his new, young, skanky home-wrecker girlfriend in the car, who sees the ex-wife and flips her the bird! *(Oh, no she didn't!)*

The origin of "Hell on wheels" apparently goes back to the wild, wild West around the 1860s in North America when an army of Union Pacific Railroad workers were building the first Transcontinental Railroad. Opportunists wanting to give these workers something to spend their hard-earned money on, rented flatcars (flat freight cars) and literally turned them into entertainment venues like mobile saloons, brothels, dance halls and gambling casinos. Religious zealots considered these activities to be the work of the devil and preached that everyone involved in this "hell on wheels" was doomed to the blazing, ever-lasting fires of the abyss. I don't know—it sounds to me more like it was "Vegas on wheels!"

This October 13th, share a few of your favorite silly saying with friends and family, and encourage them to do the same. Use this occasion for a silly team-building activity of get creative with it and create a *Silly Saying Game* for family game night! It certainly doesn't have to be anything too complicated because as a more current silly saying goes: "ain't nobody got time for dat!" So just make it simple. You could even pattern it after any one of the popular games that have stood the fun test of time like Charades or Pictionary, and easy peasy, it's time to have some fun!

*See ya later, alligator!*

# National Knock-Knock Joke Day

## Always October 31st

Knock, knock.
Who's there?
Orange.
Orange who?
Orange you glad it's Halloween?!

Who knew Halloween had a cool sidekick like *National Knock-Knock Joke Day*? OK, so "cool" may not be exactly how adults view knock-knock jokes because the word "corny" seems to be a much better fit. But, hey, Halloween is mostly for kids, and kids—

especially the little ones—think knock-knock jokes are the coolest! Knock-knock jokes are often the first kind of jokes the little munchkins learn how to tell. Best of all is the totally awesome feeling a little one gets after making others laugh with a funny knock-knock joke.

So be sure to have your smart phone cameras and videos at the ready on Halloween, and not just for showing off the little superheroes, princesses and frightfully ghoulish goblins and zombies. Be ready to capture the priceless expression on your little Wolverine's face as he (or she) shows off their stand-up-comedian abilities by making people laugh out loud at the cool knock-knock jokes they worked so hard to learn.

*Knock, knock.*
*Who's there?*
*Bean.*
*Bean who?*
*Bean waiting all day for Trick or Treat!*

Here's a collection of jokes created especially for Halloween that the whole family can have fun with throughout the day. Pick out a few to have your kid(s) memorize or write down on paper to take along, and don't forget that the preparation for a successful Halloween is half the fun!

For the Trick-or-Treaters:

Knock, knock.
Who's there?
Phillip.
Phillip who?
Phillip my bag with candy, please!
Knock, knock.
Who's there?

Norma Lee.
Norma Lee who?
Norma Lee I don't look this scary!

Knock, knock.
Who's there?
Bean.
Bean who?
Bean waiting all day for Trick or Treat!

Knock, knock.
Who's there?
Emma.
Emma who?
Emma gonna get any candy or what?!

Knock, knock.
Who's there?
Howie.
Howie who?
Howie gonna eat all this candy?!

Jokes for those on door duty:

Knock, knock.
Who's there?
Ice cream.
Ice cream who?
Ice cream whenever I see a scary monster like you!

Knock, knock.
Who's there?
Butter.
Butter who?
Butter be careful not to eat too much candy tonight!

Knock, knock.
Who's there?
Justin.
Justin who?
Justin time for lots and lots of candy!

Knock, knock.
Who's there?
Omar.
Omar who?
Omar goodness, your costume is A-Maaaa-Zing!

Knock, knock.
Who's there?
Tank.
Tank who?
You're welcome!

And here's one more, especially for you:

Knock, knock.
Who's there?
Irish.
Irish who?

*Irish You All a Happy Halloween!!*

# International Tongue Twister Day

## Always the Second Sunday in November

Hey, look at me, I'm a Tongue Twister!

## Have a Dance Party in Your Mouth on International Tongue Twister Day!

I'll bet you didn't know (*or care*) about the number of people who have the ability to *curl* their tongue. It's between 65 and 81 percent. But the number of people who have the ability to *twist* their tongue—100 percent! But seriously folks, why should you, personally, give a hoot about such trivia? Because, my friend, life's too short to only care about what's critical, when it's far more gratifying to care a little about what's trivial. Case in point: November 12th is *International Tongue Twister Day*! This wild and wacky, imitation of a holiday is dedicated to the sole purpose of twisting tongues all around the world!

Try saying this easy tongue twister as fast as you can: "Tommy Tucker and tall Tim took 10 tiny toy trucks into town on Tuesday." Pretty easy, right? Now try to say *this* one five times fast: "Unique New York." Not as easy as you thought, huh?

*How many cuckoos could a good cook cook, if a good cook could cook cuckoos?*

So as you can see, despite the statistical percentages, tongue *curling* is totally easy when compared to the coiling, contorted, crooked, and convoluted condition a good twister can cause to a person's tongue. And let's face it, tongue *curling* is endlessly boring and uninspiring. Tongue *twisting* is like there's a dance party going on in your mouth! It's like your tongue is doing the jitterbug!

On *International Tongue Twister Day*, (always the second Sunday in November), consider celebrating the day by having a tongue-twister tournament with your family, your friends, your poetry club members, or for an impromptu freestyle rap session down at the *Boys & Girls Club*. This can be fun whether it's done in person or on social media, or both. See who can correctly recite the most tongue twisters with the least amount of mistakes! Each tongue twister must be recited quickly and multiple times. Use a stopwatch for tiebreakers if it turns out you have two or more tongue-twister titans in your tournament.

Here are a few fabulously fun tongue-twister favorites that you might find useful. Saying them once may be fun and effortless, but saying them fast may be far-fetched and fairly futile:

- How many cuckoos could a good cook cook, if a good cook could cook cuckoos?

- I wish to wash my Irish wristwatch.

- Can you imagine an imaginary menagerie manager, imagining managing an imaginary menagerie?

- We all just saw six slim, sick, slick sycamore saplings.

- Betty and Barbara brought back big blue balloons from the big barn bazaar.

- Old oily Ollie oils old oily autos.

- If one doctor doctors another doctor, does the doctor who doctors the doctor doctor the way the doctor he is doctoring doctors? Or does he doctor the doctor the way the doctor who doctors doctors?

- Silly Sally swiftly shooed seven silly sheep who shilly-shallied South.

- Sheep shouldn't sleep in a shack; sheep should sleep in a shed.

- Friendly Frank flips fine flapjacks.

- Selfish shellfish.

- You know New York, you need New York, you know you need unique New York.

- Seeking shelter for six sick scenic sightseers.

- A tutor who tooted the flute
  tried to tutor two tooters to toot.
  Said the two to the tutor: "Is it tougher to toot,
  or to tutor two tooters to toot?

- What time does the wristwatch strap shop shut?

- Which wristwatches are Swiss wristwatches?

- A swan swam over the sea. Swim, swan, swim!
  The swan swam back again. Well swum, swan!

- Sinful Caesar sipped his snifter, seized his knees, and sneezed.

- Rubber baby buggy bumper.

- Betty bought some butter.
  But the butter Betty bought was bitter.
  "If I bake with this bitter butter,
  it will make my batter bitter.
  But a bit of better butter
  will make my batter better.
  So she bought a bit of butter
  that was better than her bitter butter.
  Then she baked it in her batter

and the batter was no longer bitter.
So 'twas better that Betty bought
a bit of better butter.

*Happy International Tongue Twister Day* to you all! I'm
on my way to hear some local yokels yodel.

# National Absurdity Day!

Always November 20th

**A National Day of Absurdity?**
**Now That's Absurd!**

November 20th is *National Absurdity Day*. How absurd is that? How absurd is it that there are people who purposely perpetuate and promote such peculiar and purposeless days! These people obviously have a whole lot of crazy goin' on! But for those of us who like a little *cray cray* inserted into our day-to-day, *National Absurdity Day* gives us an excuse to let loose our inner weirdo.

"Embrace the absurd" is the order of the day for this wild and wacky, fabricated impersonation of a holiday. It is a day created to encourage us to recall and note some of the ridiculously absurd things in history, in our country and in our lives. It also invites us to dive head-first into our own version of Alice in Wonderland's rabbit hole and celebrate the occasion by acting completely and outrageously absurd!

---

*Absurdity is obviously an acquired taste and is not for those who have pledged their lives to sensibility and (yawn) constraint.*

---

On the other hand, if you're clearly not interested in the art of the absurd because you consider yourself to be too ... sane, that's totally understandable. Absurdity is obviously an acquired taste and is not for those who have pledged their lives to sensibility and (yawn) constraint. Sensible people like that would rather celebrate *National Flossing Day (even bigger yawn)* which is always the day after Thanksgiving.

For those of us, however, who have pledged to live our lives to the fullest extent of wacky, we will certainly be contemplating—commemorating possibly, but definitely contemplating—*National Absurdity Day* this year in our own personal wacky way! Opinions about what constitutes absurdity are often as different as night and day, but whatever you decide to do with the opportunities this occasion presents, in the spirit of the season, be sure to keep it family-friendly and clean, and not smutty or obscene.

And speaking of absurd, there are a plethora of other days of absurdity throughout the year that deserve at least honorable mention. There are wacky-silly-loony-daffy-kooky-nutty-goofy-screwy -freaky days found in every single month—dozens of days we can choose to celebrate, commemorate or just plain contemplate.

Here's a whole year's worth of bazaar holiday imper-sonators that may actually make *National Absurdity Day* seem sort of ... sensible:

- Jan – No Pants Subway Ride Day

- Feb – Cow Milked While Flying in an Airplane Day

- Mar – What If Cats and Dogs Had Opposable Thumbs? Day

- Apr – Dog Farting Awareness Day

- May – Put a Pillow On Your Fridge Day

- Jun – Fish Are Friends Not Food! Day

- Jul – National Take Your Houseplant for a Walk Day

- Aug – Sneak Some Zucchini Onto Your Neighbor's Porch Night

- Sept – Ask A Stupid Question Day

- Oct – Worldwide Howl at the Moon Night

- Nov – National Married to a Scorpio Support Day

- Dec – Pretend to be a Time Traveler Day

Search for details on any or all of these daffy days us-ing your favorite Internet browser. But if you're still not interested in acknowledging *National Absurdity Day* this November 20th, that's perfectly understandable. And besides, there's always the option of celebrating a different absurd-worthy observance later that same week. It's called *All Our Uncles Are Monkeys Day!* Now that sounds like a day of absurdity with a side of monkey business!

DEC

# Prohibition Repeal Day

## Every December 5th Since 1933

### 13 Intoxicating Facts
### About the 13 Years of Prohibition

As far as wild and wacky days in history go, December 5, 1933 was a occasion that probably turned into one of the wildest celebrations in American History! That was the day the Federal Government finally came to its senses and repealed Prohibition! For those of you who don't remember being awake during this particular chapter in your American History class, Prohibition was a "noble experiment" by the U.S. Government when booze was banned from sea to shining sea! It lasted just 13 years (1920-1933) before it was repealed.

This December 5th marks another anniversary of this happy day in history—now known as *Repeal Day*—when the 21st Amendment of the Constitution overturned the 18th Amendment of the Constitution because the 18th was an epic failure! The 18th Amendment—aka Prohibition—prohibited the manufacture, sale and transportation of intoxicating liquor.

*The government had to admit that Prohibition wasn't just an epic failure, it was an epically, phenomenal fiasco!*

Its intent was to encourage our nation to value a society of people with minds and bodies free from the undermining effects of alcohol. Someone once said, "the road to hell is paved with good intentions," and Prohibition played a huge part in keeping the highway to hell filled with the traffic of bootleggers before the government had to admit that Prohibition wasn't just an epic failure, it was an epically, phenomenal fiasco!

"There'd never been a more advantageous time to be a criminal in America than during the 13 years of Prohibition. At a stroke, the American government closed down the fifth largest industry in the United States—alcohol production—and just handed it to criminals. A pretty remarkable thing to do." ~Bill Bryson (Author)

Here's a look at 13 intoxicating facts about the 13 years of Prohibition:

1. To date, Prohibition is the only Constitutional Amendment ever revoked. That's out of 27 total Amendments and 230 years since the Constitution was instituted. Incidentally, that last amendment, the 27th, had to do with pay raises for Congress. And if you think Congress dilly-dallies and lolly-gags about getting anything done nowadays, the 27th Amendment was first proposed in 1789, but was not fully ratified until 1992! *(Wow, talk about kicking the proverbial can down the road!)*

   *Prohibition did not make it illegal to drink alcohol! (Wait, what??)*

2. Prohibition did not make it illegal to drink alcohol! *(Wait, what??)* That's right, consuming liquor was still legal. You just weren't supposed to make it or sell it or transport it.

3. Any alcohol that was purchased prior to January 17, 1920—the start of Prohibition—was legal to keep and enjoy, as long as it was done in the privacy of one's home. Wealthy cocktail drinkers purchased entire warehouses of alcohol inventories and built cavernous wine cellars, enabling them to legally be inebriated for as long as possible. Poor folks, on the other hand, were forced to turn to moonshiners for their ... *moonshine.*

4. Prohibiting liquor became so unfavorable and unacceptable among the drinking population that it

---

*Thousands of female protesters carried signs saying things like "Lips that touch liquor shall not touch ours."*

---

stirred rebellion like never before and unexpectedly made drinkers of nearly everyone. It actually became fashionable to break the law! People found all sorts of crafty ways to hide their *hooch*—including false books, hollowed out canes and hot water bottles. No other law in America has ever been violated so frequently and shamelessly by so many decent and law-abiding citizens.

5. Women's organizations played a key role in the fight in favor of Prohibition because of the belief that American men spent more money on alcohol than on their own families. Illegal drinking establishments also encouraged gambling, prostitution, tobacco use and (gasp) dancing! Fed up women rose up across the country and began a movement (the Temperance Movement) to fight against liquor's highly destructive force in marriages and families. Groups of female protesters carried signs saying things like "Lips that touch liquor shall not touch ours." *(Cheers to the power of organized nagging!)*

6. Prohibition was supposed to reduce crime, poverty and drunkenness, but despite very early signs of success, and then despite enforcement efforts by the federal, state and local officers, Prohibition

inadvertently stimulated the proliferation of rampant, widespread underground, organized criminal gangland activity.

7. The Great Depression forced "bootlegging" to become the career of choice for thousands because of the massive demands by the public for the illegal production, sale and transporting of *bathtub gin.*

8. The use of wine for religious purposes and alcohol for medicinal purposes was not prohibited under the law. Ergo, pharmacies obtained liquor licenses in order to legally distribute *rotgut,* and physicians everywhere dispensed tons of *firewater* disguised as tonics and elixirs.

*Bootleg liquor was often served in tea cups just in case there was a police raid.*

9. In the early 1920s, Chicago had more than 7,000 drinking parlors, and at its height, New York City is said to have had an estimated 30,000 of these hideaway hot spots. These mostly mob-owned establishments—called *speakeasies*—were so named because the patrons had to whisper a code word through a locked door in order to gain entrance. *Bootleg* liquor was often served in tea cups just in case there was a police raid.

10. Al Capone earned a staggering $60 million annually during his bootlegging career as America's most notorious gangster during the Prohibition era. That's about $880 million a year by today's standards, and nearly $11.5 billion total before Prohibition ended. That's more than the net worth

of Oprah, Steven Spielberg and Richard Branson combined!

11. The birth of NASCAR was a direct result of bootlegging during Prohibition! According to folklore, a bunch of dirt poor, good ol' boy moonshiners used small, souped-up vehicles to quickly deliver their *white lightning,* and to better outrun the police. When racing each other became a common practice among the drivers' thrill rides, someone decided to cut a crude race track out of a cow pasture and there you have it, stock car racing was born! For countless years since then, stock car racing has been the reigning leader as the most popular spectator sport in America.

*The birth of NASCAR was a direct result of bootlegging during Prohibition!*

12. Although on December 5, 1933, Congress finally voted to end of Prohibition, several states continued to prohibit alcohol after the repeal. It was not totally abandoned until 1966!! Fast forward to the 21st Century: "A new poll shows that only 3 percent of the population strongly approve of the job Congress is doing. With a margin of error of 4 percent, it's quite possible that 'less than no one' thinks Congress is doing a good job." ~Jay Leno

13. By 1932, the country was deeply mired in the Great Depression and the need for tax revenue and job creation made the idea of legalizing the liquor industry a no brainer for presidential candidates like Franklin D. Roosevelt. Using the repeal of Prohibition as a platform during the election, FDR's victory was easy. At 4:31pm on Repeal Day, December 5, 1933, President Roosevelt is said to have

signed the 21st Amendment, and then hoisted a dirty martini high in the air for a toast to the end of prohibition by declaring: "What America needs now is a drink!"

Much like the supporters of Prohibition, many people nowadays still think America is going to pot. And to commemorate *Prohibition Repeal Day* this year, at 4:31pm on December 5th, many eager supporters of this unprecedented repeal will be hoisting another prohibited intoxicant high into the air and proposing a new toast: *"What America needs now is a joint!"*

# Cat Herders Day

## Always December 15th

Hey, Fly Boys! You herded us into these silly poses, now stop with the photobombs!

## A Stress-Free Christmas and Flying Pigs: All Possible on Cat Herders Day!

For many of us, especially women, and more especially for women with children, we all tend to believe that a stress-free Christmas is totally possible ... when pigs fly! Then and only then, when we personally witness Porky and his posse of piglets flying across the sky like Santa's reindeer, only then will you be convinced that it's possible to have a stress-free holiday season. Well, believe it or not, every year on December 15th, *Cat Herders Day* arrives *(that's right, you heard me, I said "Cat Herders Day")* to give us hope that, although managing our lives during the Christmas Holiday Season can be like herding cats *(Impossible!)*, *Cat Herders Day* is the day ... that could be *the* day ... when pigs fly!

Imagine this: An extraordinary day when it might actually be possible for the spirit of Christmas to deliver its special gifts to all our hearts through feelings of *Joy to the World, Peace on Earth* and *Good Will Toward Men*, WITHOUT all the excessive stress and distress that invariably invades our not-always-happy holidays. Enter *Cat Herders Day*—a day

*Cat Herders Day — a day that's all about the possibility of impossibilities!*

that's all about the possibility of impossibilities! Pigs get to fly and "the twelfth of never" shows up for the first time ever!

*Cat Herders Day* was created to give even the busiest of us, the opportunity, the encouragement, and the inspiration to prove to ourselves and/or others that, if put to the task, we know we can always call upon our inner super-hero to step up and help conquer whatever it is that needs conquering. You know, like during emergencies when women have been known to lift cars off babies or when they have to successfully survive the most treacherous Black Friday shopping spree in the history of Christmas shopping. *Cat Herders Day* is a day to believe not only in Christmas miracles, but to believe in ourselves. To believe that being able to do the impossible in our lives is not only conceivable, but achievable!

Example: Think you can't actually herd cats? Guess again because "yes, you can!" Simply take a bag of cat treats, shake it, and watch as a bunch of finicky little felines toss their uppity cat-titudes to the curb and come trotting towards you. Or, purr-haps you might

---

*"Nothing is impossible. The word itself says 'I'm possible.'"* ~Audrey Hepburn

---

prefer to use the Hansel and Gretel method of dropping treats like they were breadcrumbs and watch while Mrs. Flossie and all her feisty little fur balls litter-ally follow you like you're the Piped Piper. "Nothing is impossible. The word itself says 'I'm possible.'" ~Audrey Hepburn

This December 15th, pay tribute to *Cat Herders Day* by strategizing and making plans to avert a cat-astrophic Christmas. Make some of those impossibilities paw-sible by utilizing your purr-ticular "bag of treats" to not only help you survive and enjoy this purr-ecious holiday season, but to manage the un-manageable chaos that is your life this time of year. Like having to shop 'til you drop while enduring long lines and huge crowds of crazy people. Like having to spend, spend, spend 'til your funds are at an end, then bake and decorate 'til every bone in your body aches. Like trying to conquer the constant cravings to eat a ton of sweets, causing you to gain a ton of weight, until you qualify as freight.

Then there are the office parties, filled with intoxicated co-workers, or worse yet, your mate's office party with his/her inebriated boss who keeps winking at you. This is also the season for the visits from the loud and loony, overly-opinionated relatives who you love because they're family, but who you can't bring yourself to like.

*May the Lord have mercy on your overly-stressed-battered-and-tattered-and-not-so-merry soul!*

Top that all off with the enormous amount of stress that comes with traveling, then double that stress if you travel with young children. Or the epically overwhelming anxiety that comes with having to see and interact with your ex and his/her new family ... after a bitter divorce. May the Lord have mercy on your overly-stressed-battered-and-tattered-and-not-so-merry soul!

But there's no need to fear, my fur-ends, for *Cat Herders Day* can rein all that insanity in! All the madness in your life can miraculously become manageable once you put on your super-hero mindset and shake your big ol' bag of treats. Christmas miracles ain't got nothin' on the mini-miracles, or even the many miracles you might manage to pull off this year! *(Insert crowd cheering here.)*

Once you're done with all that, if you're still feeling pumped up on all that miraculous energy and confidence, and still able to leap tall buildings in a single bound after the holidays, try your hand at a few other im-paws-ibilities like these:

- See if you can stay off Santa's naughty list this year.

- Devise a way to pay off the national debt.

- Teach your goldfish how to speak Spanish.

- Find an honest politician.

- Make your dog stop licking himself.

- Lick your own elbow.

- Say "Unique New York" five times fast.

- Give a convincing explanation to your kids about why Santa only works one day a year and then spends the rest of the year judging them.

- Make a top 10 list of things to love about Justin Beiber.

- Drive the speed limit ... all the time.

- Tickle yourself.

- Read the entire Terms and Conditions of any online contract.

- Guarantee the world that Kim and Kanye will stay together forever.

*Cat Herders Day* is more than just a day devoted to seeing if we can make pigs fly when we really need them to. It was also designed to help de-stress more than just our holiday season by encouraging people to celebrate *Cat Herders Day* by adopting a cat or kitten! The power of the purr has not only been medically proven to be relaxing, it is said to reduce one's chance of heart attack by 40 percent ... Purr-iceless!

*Now go forth and succeed in having an Amazingly Happy Christmas and a Super Merry New Year.*

\* \* \*

# *Epilogue*

And speaking of having an Amazingly Happy Christmas and a Super Merry New Year, don't put this book down just yet because it's reusable for the New Year! Flip back through the pages to January and fold down the corners of some of the days of wonder that intrigue you the most or put stickies on the ones that you feel most compelled to share with others. Then be sure to mark your calendar so you can plan ahead for the makings of what could really become an epically awesome month and year because of all the Wild and Wacky Holiday-*ish* Occasions that you now know you want to celebrate, commemorate, or just plain contemplate!

# About the Author

Rita Beck is a freelance "amusement writer" who specializes in news you can use to amuse. She has a passion for writing to delight, entertain and lift the spirits of her readers. By day, this married, baby-boomer, bi-racial*, grandmother of five, works in a Financial Advisor's office in Southern Wisconsin. By night, this Dave Barry wannabe, who was first inspired by Erma Bombeck, writes and blogs about wild and wacky holiday-*ish* days.

Raised in Chicago, Rita's resume includes jobs ranging from Producer for an old radio program called, "Talkin' with Truckers;" to Administrative Assistant for 12 crazy corporate consultants; to Website Creator (formally known as TheBoomerBunch.com, about Baby Boomers making it cool to grow old); to her most favorite past job, Substitute Tap Dance Teacher.

Always the glass-half-full sort, Rita likes to spend time on the golf course with her husband, Eric, as they fantasize about the day they can both retire. This book is her first venture into self-publishing and she hopes you enjoy it.

Feel free to send comments, compliments or critiques to: rbeck516@yahoo.com.

*Had to give a shout-out to the mulattos of the world because Megan Markle just married her Prince Harry and has made it unbelievably cool to be bi-racial! We are the result of Blacks and Whites coming together to create beings who were born to unite others. People are always quoting "Be the change you wish to see in the world." Bi-racial individuals are living examples of the change so many others wish to see in the world. I'm not saying that we should blend all the races because diversity is very important, but for those who do blend with another race, the resulting children become far more diverse as individuals. Just a little food for thought, y'all.*

# Index

## 33 Annual Wild & Wacky
## Holiday-*ish* Occasions
## And Their Twitter Hashtags

*(If you can't find it on Twitter, that's your cue*
*to start it up and make it happen!)*